Changing the Guard in Brussels

THE WASHINGTON PAPERS

. . . intended to meet the need for an authoritative, yet prompt, public appraisal of the major developments in world affairs.

President, CSIS: David M. Abshire

Series Editor: Walter Laqueur

Director of Publications: Nancy B. Eddy

Managing Editor: Donna R. Spitler

MANUSCRIPT SUBMISSION

The Washington Papers and Praeger Publishers welcome inquiries concerning manuscript submissions. Please include with your inquiry a curriculum vitae, synopsis, table of contents, and estimated manuscript length. Manuscripts must be between 120–200 double-spaced typed pages. All submissions will be peer reviewed. Submissions to *The Washington Papers* should be sent to *The Washington Papers*; The Center for Strategic and International Studies; 1800 K Street NW; Suite 400; Washington, DC 20006. Book proposals should be sent to Praeger Publishers; One Madison Avenue; New York NY 10010.

Changing the Guard in Brussels

An Insider's View of the EC Presidency

Guy de Bassompierre

Foreword by Robert E. Hunter

Published with The Center for
Strategic and International Studies
Washington, D.C.

PRAEGER

New York
Westport, Connecticut
London

Library of Congress Cataloging-in-Publication Data

De Bassompierre, Guy.
  Changing the guard in Brussels : an insider's view of the EC
presidency / Guy de Bassompierre.
    p. cm. — (The Washington papers, ISSN 0278-937X ; vol. XVI,
135)
  "Published with the Center for Strategic and International
Studies, Washington, D.C."
  Includes index.
  ISBN 0-275-93186-2 (alk. paper). ISBN 0-275-93187-0 (pbk. : alk.
paper)
  1. European communities. 2. European federation. 3. European
Economic Community Council of Ministers. I. Center for Strategic
and International Studies (Washington, D.C.) II. Title.
III. Series: Washington papers ; 135.
JN15.D38 1988
341.24′2 — dc19   88-23580

The *Washington Papers* are written under the auspices of The Center
for Strategic and International Studies (CSIS) and published
with CSIS by Praeger Publishers. The views expressed in these papers
are those of the authors and not necessarily those of the Center.

Library of Congress Catalog Card Number: 88-23580
ISBN: 0-275-93186-2 (cloth)
         0-275-93187-0 (paper)

First published in 1988

Praeger Publishers, One Madison Avenue, New York, NY 10010
An imprint of Greenwood Publishing Group, Inc.

Printed in the United States of America

∞

The paper used in this book complies with the Permanent
Paper Standard issued by the National Information Standards
Organization (Z39.48-1984).

10   9   8   7   6   5   4   3   2

Contents

Foreword

During an existence of more than three decades, the European Community (EC) has gone from being a limited exercise in the functional coordination of some economic activities of six West European states to being a principal engine and organizer of an expanding integration of twice that many countries. In 1958, three separate communities for coal and steel, economics, and atomic energy were blazing trails in the wilderness; now the landscape is thoroughly developed, and the European experiment can be said to have well and truly succeeded. And a date on the calendar—1992—has come to symbolize a major leap forward for Europe. If all goes well, on or about that time the European Community will implement the Single European Act, which will bring down the last barriers to the creation of a single market embracing more than 320 million people.

The implications of 1992 have hardly been grasped—indeed, they will go far beyond the economic consequences of creating such an enormous trading entity, the largest in the world. The political ramifications will also be significant, spurring on efforts to develop political and other supranational institutions. In time, these could entail a fully fledged foreign and defense personality for the 12 nations—or more, by the time it happens. In effect, 1992 represents a renewal of the act of faith that produced the early communities. Although largely economic in declared purpose, the Single European Act still does not lose sight of the underlying inspiration for integration from its inception: to use functional devices to serve political ends, especially one that has now been so taken for granted that it exists largely beneath the consciousness of most Europeans – the prevention of another great intra-European war.

During the many years that the European Community has been developing, most Americans have focused on other factors in Europe, primarily under the heading of security. Other institutions, especially the North Atlantic Treaty Organization, have been more important. Indeed, most U.S. observers, other than those professionally caught up in trade, tend to pay more attention to ancillary European institutional developments – such as the Western European Union or the so-called Eurogroup of defense ministers – rather than to the formal institutions of the Community. While not exactly terrae incognitae, understanding of them in the United States is largely limited to a few political science specialists and those individuals whose direct livelihood depends on working with the EC bureaucracy in Brussels.

But as the Community gradually takes on a greater political personality and assumes more power and authority for regulating day-to-day economic relations between European countries and the outside world, a new premium has been placed on understanding just how it works. At the economic level, 1992 will bring about changes that will create two classes of foreign economic entities in regard to the European Community: those that are "in" and those that are "out." In the politics that relate to economics, there will increasingly be an answer to Henry Kissinger's famous question, to whom does one talk in "Europe"? It will slowly become a group of individuals at the Berlaymont in Brussels. European Political Cooperation, a modest effort from the 1970s to give the Community states some limited capacity to discuss a limited range of foreign policy issues – mostly the Middle East and the Conference on Security and

Cooperation in Europe (the Helsinki Process)–will also be expanded.

Not for now, perhaps, will there be anything even remotely approaching a United States of Europe, but no longer will any American sensitive to his country's relations with the countries of Western Europe be able to ignore what is happening at the Community's hub in Brussels as well as at the ends of the spokes, such as the European Parliament in Strasbourg. For decades, U.S. observers with strong Atlanticist inclinations have talked about the creation of a second "pillar" to the Western alliance, although most have been ambivalent about the development of such a pillar where it could lead to a European independence of action, method, or even goals–in whatever field. But whether Americans like it or not, developments within the European Community, plus the promise of 1992–however long that named event actually takes to arrive–mean that getting to know this congeries of European institutions has become a matter of far more than passing interest.

Yet so little has been said or written about how the European Community actually works! There is no single source to which one can repair, no collective wisdom set down as a primer or guide to the workings of the complex set of political and bureaucratic relations that increasingly guide the economic destiny–and in time the political destiny as well–of so many West Europeans. In part, this lack derives from the youth of the Community's institutions. Knowledge can only be built upon experience–that is, upon what really happens, as opposed to what is set down in the Treaty of Rome and other documents–and this depends on some practitioners coming forward to tell what they and their colleagues actually do, and how, and why.

This volume, *Changing the Guard in Brussels*, thus opens a door to a world that has been there but only seen "through a glass darkly." It pretends to be about the presidency of the European Community–the rotating leadership of the European Council of Ministers, the representation of national governments rather than supranational institutions–but it is so much more than that. In the following pages is to be found a guide to the practical workings of the whole institution of the Community in its many parts. As such, it lays out a dimension of understanding that has hitherto been lacking, but which henceforth will be indispensable for anyone who wants to know how "Brussels" – in truth, "Europe" – actually works. It also illuminates what is probably the principal tension within the Community – that between the integrating of a single market, a single economic entity, eventually a single political personality, and the centripetal forces that are represented by the 12 member countries and their continuing, natural reluctance to cede precious sovereignty over the shaping of their individual futures.

Changing the Guard could hardly have found an author more able to write it. Guy de Bassompierre has both gifts and opportunities, each essential to a project of this importance. Well-trained as a scholar and diplomat, Guy has gifts of insight into things far beyond his native Belgium – indeed, as one of a breed of young "Europeans" who have never before existed – and a felicity of phrase and description in all of his many languages. Combined with his well-developed capacity for both acting and understanding – in a word, wisdom – he has also had opportunity: service within and in liaison to the institutions of the European Community, responsibility for managing what happens, working with others as they have mastered their own tasks. In short, he has been a rare blend of organizer, operator, and observer.

In a few pages, this volume provides the key to so much of what needs to be known about the presidency of the European Council, and it tantalizes with insights on the other Community institutions. It presages, and sharpens the appetite for, more writing by the same author on similar subjects.

Robert E. Hunter
Director of European Studies
Center for Strategic and International Studies

July 1988

About the Author

Guy de Bassompierre is minister counselor (economic and commercial) at the Belgian Embassy in Washington, D.C. Most recently he was a visiting scholar at the Center for Strategic and International Studies (1987–1988). Previously he served as adviser on European affairs to the Belgian minister of external relations. He has also served as assistant to Belgium's representative to the EC, as head of the European Political Cooperation Section of the Belgian Foreign Ministry, and as head of the economic section of the Belgian Embassy in Madrid. Dr. de Bassompierre holds a Ph.D. in law from the Université Catholique de Louvain.

Preface

This volume, written while I was a visiting fellow at the Center for Strategic and International Studies in Washington, D.C., is the outgrowth of a shorter essay prepared for the Center as a guide for Americans interested in the process of European integration. It does not attempt to be a scholarly dissertation on the merits and shortcomings of the Presidency, but rather it is an insider's appraisal of the institutions of the European Community as seen by someone familiar with the daily activity of the Council of Ministers. It thus deals with the reality rather than with the ideal and results from personal experience, not from an academic study.

Watching the tortuously slow process of European integration in recent years has been akin to watching grass grow. Twelve European powers, most of whom have had a taste of global dominion in the past, are understandably reluctant to forsake their traditional sovereignty. But a process is under way that is beginning to acquire a new momentum, especially with the 1992 deadline so close. By that date, all EC internal barriers are slated to come down, ensuring the free flow of persons, goods, and capital. European union, if ever achieved, will have profound political, economic, and security consequences for the world at large.

U.S. policymakers should notice what is happening and what it could portend.

Regardless of the outcome, however, the process is a unique and absorbing experiment in supranationality. Nothing quite like it has ever before been attempted. This book therefore is in reality a story about 320 million free and prosperous people reaching for the next stage of European evolution. Despite its moments of comic relief, such a serious and historic adventure is likely to have worldwide impact.

My thanks are extended to the Center for Strategic and International Studies, which provided me with a congenial and intellectually stimulating environment. A special expression of gratitude is owed to John Q. Blodgett, former U.S. foreign service officer and fellow at CSIS, for the invaluable help he gave me by providing a first, vigorous, and experienced U.S. reaction to the text, as well as by eliminating some of the more glaring gallicisms in the manuscript. All of the views expressed are strictly my own and in no way represent any official attitude.

Washington, D.C.
June 1988

Summary

In 1992 Europe will in all likelihood achieve its goal of dismantling the border controls between its 12 member states. A vast, integrated market of 320 million consumers will appear, presenting both a challenge and an opportunity for U.S. businessmen, investors, exporters, and officials.

Most Americans, however, do not know how the European Community works. Who makes the decisions? What are the different roles of the European Commission and of the Council of Ministers? Are there security implications in the emergence of the single European market? What are the prospects for U.S.-EC relations? This volume leads the reader through the EC mechanisms in an attempt to present them fully, yet simply enough to be understood by a wide range of professionals and students whose activities expose them to European integration. The author approaches the subject from the perspective of a member state discharging its six months' turn at the helm of the EC Council of Ministers.

Written specifically for an American public, this book is the first to present the interaction of the various European decision makers in easy-to-understand terms. It draws upon many examples to illustrate the achievements and the failures of European integration, ending with perspectives for the future.

Introduction

The European Community (EC) does not yet carry the political clout one could expect from this conglomerate of 12 European nations with a population of 322 million and a combined gross national product (GNP) close to that of the United States. Not a federation or a confederation, but more than a mere customs union, it is usually viewed as an economic giant but a political dwarf. Yet, the EC already plays a lead negotiating role in several major international conferences, such as the recent Uruguay trade round of the General Agreement on Tariffs and Trade (GATT).

At the same time, the EC's internal mechanisms and institutions are not well known, except by a few specialists. One of its more important decision-making mechanisms, the Presidency of the Council of Ministers, rotates every six months among its 12 member states. Regardless of its size or influence, each member state has the chance to hold the office every six years. Foreign government and business negotiators are often frustrated or baffled by this carousel. To their detriment, they often fail to appreciate the relative significance of the shifting Presidency and its correct place in the complicated European institutional process. Typically most people either overemphasize the Presidency, or they underestimate its role. Conflicting interests built into the

European institutional process certainly help explain these mistakes. One of the purposes of this volume is thus to try to clarify the role of the EC Presidency. Such an examination is intended to give the reader not only an insider's view of the EC, but also an awareness of the ongoing process of European political integration.

The European Community has evolved rapidly from its beginning in 1951 as the European Coal and Steel Community, expanding in 1957 to include the European Economic Community (EEC) and the European Atomic Energy Community (EURATOM). Also known more prosaically as the Common Market, especially in the United Kingdom (UK), which mainly emphasizes the economic aspect of European integration, its official title is either the European Communities or the European Community. Both titles, plural or singular, are used interchangeably, mirroring the institutional and political changes that have been taking place in the ongoing process of European integration.

The EC has grown from its original core of 6 member states to the present 12, and more applicants, declared or potential, are waiting in the wings.[1] Its responsibilities – no longer limited to coal and steel – cover such diverse fields as technology, international trade, development aid, and agriculture. Already the world's major trading power, the EC has also developed an instrument to coordinate foreign policy that could become a global influence. The EC is moving closer to assuming monetary responsibilities, and the day cannot be too far off when security and defense matters will be addressed collectively by its member states, whether within or outside the EC framework.[2] The present U.S. strategic umbrella over Western Europe may not last forever in a fast-changing world.

The EC's presidential rotation is more than a semiannual routine crew change. Each member state is acutely conscious of the opportunities provided by its fleeting chairmanship to press its own desiderata. Each government structures its agenda differently from that of its predecessors or its successors. The intensity of its commitments to

European integration varies, as does its preoccupations with the external policies of the 12 member states (the Twelve). Broadly speaking, Italy and the Benelux countries (*BE*lgium, the *NE*therlands, and *LUX*embourg), for example, have been consistent proponents of greater integration up to now, whereas Denmark or the UK have put greater emphasis on the intergovernmental approach. These attitudes are not as clearcut, however, in the case of a difficult, specific issue, when integrationists and intergovernmentalists might behave out of character and break the pattern.

This volume also examines the changing U.S.-EC relationship. Most people would agree that, close as it is, this relationship of 40 years is today under strain and must be nurtured to be preserved. Old assumptions will not long remain valid if no recognition is given to the many evolving realities on both sides of the Atlantic. One of them – European integration – is likely to become more important in the context of a possible reshaping of NATO toward an alliance made up of two equal pillars. The European arm of NATO lacks a full-scale coordinating body of its own. Could the EC become the institutional framework for the European pillar? Although this question is legitimate, it cannot yet be answered. But, whatever the outcome, the Presidency and the Council of Ministers will play a major role in the evolving redefinition of the transatlantic relationship. Three successive presidencies have addressed this question in the recent past. The acceleration of the dialogue between the superpowers will probably add impetus to this debate. New roles for the Presidency could emerge, or traditional ones could take on an added relevance. Either way, it seems to be in the best interests of the United States to follow and encourage these developments and, in so doing, to breathe new life into a different, but possibly stronger, relationship.

To understand the tasks of the Presidency requires some familiarity with the workings of the EC. Chapter 1 provides a basic description before later chapters address the running of an EC Presidency in its main spheres of responsibility: the Council of Ministers and its Committee of Permanent Representatives, European Political Cooperation and its Political Committee, the European Council (formerly known as the European Summits), and the European Parliament. Further attention is paid to the weight borne by any government entrusted with the running of the Presidency as well as to the various approaches to conducting it. The relevance to relations with the United States will be discussed before describing the passing of the baton to the next Presidency and considering possible future developments in the context of a European Union.

1

The EC Institutions:
A Basic Description

To what extent is European political integration desirable? This basic question elicits two different responses from the peoples of the EC. Some say they seek a federation of sovereign states merely to achieve a customs union and an expanded free-trade zone. Others wish to enhance their respective national sovereignties by pooling them within a European Union. Speaking in broad generalities, the perimeter states (Denmark, Greece, and the UK) prefer the first alternative, while the heartland states (the Benelux countries, France, Germany, Italy) press for the second, more visionary approach. This fundamental dichotomy of ultimate purpose has shaped the internal EC debate from its very beginnings. It is probably fair to assume that, unless the perimeter states have a change of heart – and there are signs of gradual evolution – the EC must either adopt a differentiated integration (the so-called two-speed Europe) or settle for a limited one.

A well-known figure to U.S. leaders of both the wartime and immediate postwar generations was Jean Monnet, the Frenchman from Cognac who inspired the major movement toward integration. He systematically promoted the supranational approach because of his past experience with the supply and war efforts of the Allies during both world wars. A common purpose was best served, in his view, by harnessing the imagination and dedication of the individuals involved in institutions geared to the attaining of a common goal. His most often cited sentence is both a resumé of his thinking and the creed of most European integrationists: "Nous ne coalisons pas des états, nous unissons des hommes" (We do not aim to coalesce states but to unite people).[3]

States, however, are a particularly resilient breed. One does not just do away with entities that have been around for many centuries and have grown or shrunk during hundreds of years through constant competition and near constant confrontation. Although a late phenomenon, nationalism added a formidable underpinning to the legitimacy of the state.[4] It has been discredited in Europe because of the two world wars, which many enlightened Europeans describe as one great civil war, interrupted by an uneasy 20-year truce. But nationalism has never died out. And as memories of its bitter fruits fade, it manages at least to hold its own successfully against its mortal enemy, integration.

National politicians and, above all, national civil servants are reluctant to transfer significant portions of their powers to the European institutions. One has only to compare the substantial supranational powers afforded to the High Authority of the European Coal and Steel Community in 1951 with the reduced powers given to the Commission of the EEC in 1957 to see the truth of this. Battered states, fearful of Soviet intervention in the early 1950s, were more willing to transfer powers to a common institution than those same states six years later, bolstered by the effects of the Marshall Plan and willing to embark upon colonial ventures such as Suez or Algeria. EC institutions thus are very much the result of compromise between integration and nationalism, as will become apparent from the description of the main institutional actors on the EC scene.

The Commission of the European Community

Unofficially known simply as "the Commission," the Commission of the European Community is the successor of the former High Authority set up by the 1951 Paris Treaty and of the EEC and EURATOM Commissions established by the 1957 Treaty of Rome. The Commission is an independent, supranational body currently made up of 17 members drawn from the 12 member states.[5] The oath of office, administered by the president of the European Court of Justice, stipulates that members will act independently and accept no national instructions.[6]

The Commission was devised to balance the Council of Ministers. The former is meant to defend the common European interest, while the latter can be relied upon also to represent strictly national viewpoints. The members of the Commission act as a college, and decisions are reached by the Commission as a whole, usually with a vote. Individually though, commissioners are entrusted with "portfolios" and are thus in charge of managing the sectors attributed to them. This includes the primary responsibility for drafting proposals that, after Commission approval, will be submitted to the Council of Ministers.

The president of the Commission is the first among equals. Appointed by a consensus of the member states acting at the level of prime ministers, he is selected several months before taking office, usually at the June session of the European Council—the semiannual meeting of the EC prime ministers not to be confused with the monthly meetings of the EC Council of Ministers—for a two-year renewable mandate starting on the first of January of the following year. An unwritten rule has been that the Presidency of the Commission alternates between smaller and larger member states. So far the Commission has had at least one president from each of the six founding member states and one from the UK.[7]

The president-designate then tours the capitals of the

member states with the intention of getting better ac-
quainted – if necessary – with the political and economic
leaders, of exchanging ideas about European policy, and
also of trying to influence the current government in the
choice of the one or two commissioners it will appoint to his
team in Brussels. Although some prime ministers will be
more willing than others to give a sympathetic hearing to
the future president's prudently expressed wishes on that
score, most will decide either to appoint new commissioners
or to renew the mandate of an incumbent, primarily on the
basis of national considerations. The habit of appointing
former or serving ministers to Brussels has become widely
generalized, although there are still a few limited exceptions. The existence of different coalitions in the 12 EC capitals ensure that the main political currents all have some
representation in the Commission.

One of the more eventful moments in the life of the new
Commission is the meeting during which portfolios are ap-
portioned among them. Some of the more perceptive observers of the Brussels scene have called it "the night of the
long knives" for obvious reasons. The president usually
knows fairly well whom he would like to see serving in what
capacity. Implementing his wishes is the first and daunting
test of his future authority over his peers. Opposing some of
his designs will be a combination of the national governments, any one of which may consider that only *its* commissioner can be entrusted with this or that major portfolio,
and of the personal ambitions – and also the limitations – of
his colleagues. It is very much to the credit of the current
president, Jacques Delors, that he has managed to establish his team smoothly and to avoid some of the more dramatic, even unruly, tensions of previous similar occasions.

The Commission is a powerful institution, but it could
become even more powerful. Some of its critics take it to
task for not fully exploiting its potential powers, for being
too attentive and subservient to the wishes of the governments as expressed either directly or in the Council. Its
main source of strength comes from the exclusive right it

has to introduce EC legislation. This monopoly enables it to determine both the direction and the pace of the European policy. The Council will decide whether or not to implement the Commission's proposals, but it cannot act in the absence of a proposal. If the Council wants to reject or alter a proposal, it must do so unanimously; the chances of this happening are virtually nil, especially now that there are 12 member states with different preoccupations. The Commission also usually goes through an extensive preliminary consultation process with experts drawn from the relevant groups in the member states — government officials, business and trade union leaders, consumers, and other special interests — before introducing any major new legislation or proposing any substantial departure from the existing one. This legislative monopoly explains why the Commission often describes itself as the motor that drives European integration.

Beyond this fundamental power, the Commission may be delegated further authority by the Council. In practice, a substantial extension of its powers has accrued in this fashion, especially in the Common Agricultural Policy. It is also entrusted by treaty with the negotiations with third countries, and from that provision of the treaty the Commission has managed to establish, if not exactly an empire, at least an impressive domain.[8] So extensive has it become, in fact, that no fewer than three commissioners are in charge of a part of the external relations in the present Commission.

Another substantial field of responsibility comes from its role as the "guardian of the treaties" — that is, chiefly in charge of curbing any abuse and repressing any infraction of the treaty, mostly through injunctions, the levying of fines, and the right to put a case to the European Court of Justice. To enable them to discharge all of these functions, the commissioners are supported by a large, competent, and dedicated permanent administration, staffed by nationals from the 12 member states, who have managed to work remarkably well together. The quality of this elite civil ser-

vice is high, the occasional exception only serving to reinforce this general rule. With about 10,000 employees, 20 to
25 percent of whom are interpreters or translators, the services of the Commission have reached a productivity level
unmatched by any national civil service in the EC.

From this brief description, one can thus deduce that
the Commission is as closely akin to an executive body as
one can imagine in the present unfinished phase of European integration.

The Council of Ministers

Ministers are delegated by the governments of the member
states to form the Council of Ministers, the other major
actor in the decision-making process of the EC. In addition,
the Commission is represented by one of its members. The
Council essentially has a decision-making power that often
results in legislation applicable to all member states.[9] Decisions are made unanimously or by majority voting, simple
or qualified, according to treaty provisions.[10] These provisions have recently been modified to make way for more
majority voting in those areas vitally needed to achieve the
goal of a truly integrated single market by the end of 1992.[11]
Even before this decision, though, the practice of voting
had increasingly been followed as membership grew. Some
of the hard feelings stemming from the 1966 row between
France and its five other partners over majority voting also
had begun to subside.[12]

The Council of Ministers is one of the major EC institutions that furthers European integration, which it does
whenever it adopts legislation to that end. But its membership makes it far more sensitive than the Commission to
the defense of the national interests of the member states.
Ministers are elected politicians, sensitive to the often contradictory wishes of their electorate at large and of the numerous lobbies and special interest groups that are such a
prominent feature of modern democracies. With 12 member
states present around the table, at least one government

will nearly always be facing an electoral challenge of one kind or another. The effects of local assembly elections in Bavaria will be felt in advance, as will the French municipal elections or regional elections in Italy. Well-organized and articulate national lobbies will express their preoccupations to the Council, sometimes in a spectacular fashion, as was the case when farmers actually coaxed a reluctant cow into the thirteenth-floor meeting room of the Council of Ministers' Charlemagne building in Brussels.

Just below the ministerial level sits a powerful organ, the Committee of Permanent Representatives, known by its French acronym, COREPER. Its members are the ambassadors who head these missions, with the title of permanent representatives, and a senior civil servant from the Commission. Commissioners themselves often put in appearances at particularly important COREPER meetings. COREPER has the responsibility to decide which issues are submitted to the Council of Ministers and to steer them toward the appropriate council. This considerable power has spawned criticism by partisans of European integration and members of the European Parliament, wary of what they see as a group of national officials hatching low common-denominator solutions based on intergovernmental deals far removed from their supranational ideal. The criticism reflects understandable impatience with the slow pace of European integration. It is also partially accurate. COREPER does indeed sometimes come up with waffled answers to problems arising from widely diverging national interests.

Yet COREPER does try to reach acceptable compromises and to confront ministers with politically significant alternatives. Over the years, a remarkable degree of companionship has blossomed among its long-serving members. Some ministers describe this as complicity in the wrongful bending of unrealistic national instructions to accommodate a commonsense solution acceptable to the majority.

COREPER sits at the top of a pyramid of numerous working groups of the Council that will scrutinize every Commission proposal and report their progress and findings to COREPER. They are staffed by specialists from the large missions of the member states, as well as by civil servants who fly into Brussels from their respective capitals. The working groups, of which there are dozens, work with great deliberation. As is the case in Council and COREPER meetings, a Commission representative is present and active in the working groups, defending the Commission's proposal and adapting it in case of need.

Throughout the whole process of scrutiny of a Commission proposal by the Council working at its three levels, national administrations will have had the opportunity of crossing swords with the Commission. Compromises must permanently be drawn up that reflect the ongoing tension between supranational and national interests. National interests also often conflict with one another, which is becoming more frequent since the EC doubled its membership. Both the Commission and the Presidency must play an active role in the constant search for compromises. Any president who genuinely wants to achieve progress in a particular sector will ensure that COREPER breathes down the relevant working group's neck. But it will also secure determined support from the Commission, as well as from some other member states. And it will put into place an active and capable working group chairman.

The Council of Ministers, in addition to the permanent missions of the member states, is also assisted by a very competent international staff, the General Secretariat of the Council. This staff provides the Council and the Presidency with efficient support that ranges from highly respected legal advice and the drawing up of summaries and briefs to the more routine and logistical, but essential, tasks of organizing meetings anywhere in the world. Members of the Council Secretariat are present in all meetings to help the Presidency exercise its functions.

It is a unique feature among international or supranational institutions that the Presidency of the Council, of COREPER, and of very nearly every single working group rotates by alphabetical order every six months among the member states. This rotation process affects both EC efficiency and EC relations with third countries, as will become more apparent in later chapters.

Before turning to the next major European institution – the European Parliament – the dynamic interplay between the Commission and the Council, which the treaties have established, should be stressed. Both bodies are indispensable to the functioning of the EC. Belgian Foreign Minister Léo Tindemans compared this tandem to the heraldic dual-headed eagle emblem of the Hapsburgs and spoke of the remarkable foresight of the drafters of the European treaties. Indeed, without a body such as the Commission, European integration might very well lead nowhere. By their nature hostile to political integration, national governments much prefer traditional intergovernmental cooperation. This limited approach certainly cannot sustain a sufficiently strong common purpose to keep the EC member states firmly on their course. The Commission acts not only as the driving force, but also as the common conscience, reminding everyone of the final goal, however distant. Its occasional failures in this role have only served to highlight even more the need for an active, determined, and independent body.

On the other hand, it would have been both unrealistic and irresponsible to let the Commission bear the sole responsibility for promoting European integration. A supranational administration, even one controlled by the European Parliament, simply does not have the political responsibility that rests with the national governments. Had it been alone, the Commission might have run the risk of proposing legislation that was unwanted, unnecessary, or unrealistic, whatever the thoroughness of its preliminary consultations. Indeed, even in the present system, there have been some instances of this – albeit very limited. Unconnected from the daily give and take of internal politics, the Commission could also have fallen into the trap of bureaucratic arrogance, with disastrous results.

So the founding fathers must, indeed, be credited with a degree of genius for having devised the institutional balance between Commission and Council. This is good political alchemy, even though conditions sometimes prevent it from functioning as it should – usually when someone tries to bend the rules or refuses to follow them. When the European train then derails, some effort is required to get it running again on the parallel tracks provided by the Commission and the Council.

The European Parliament

The founders of European integration stated very clearly that they were pursuing a political goal, even though they started with limited objectives. The original treaties thus provided for a parliamentary assembly. Its initial membership was drawn from the parliaments of the member states, which appointed some of their members to sit in the assembly and thus hold two mandates simultaneously. The treaties also explicitly stated that direct elections to this assembly were one of their future objectives.[13] European elections were held for the first time in 1979. Most of the major European political figures were present in a great show of enthusiasm for what was hailed as a significant step forward along the road to European unity.

The push for a greater role for the assembly had already begun earlier, resulting in additional budgetary powers in the early 1970s when it also took the symbolically significant step of calling itself the European Parliament. Its members are known, in the British fashion, as MEPs – members of the European Parliament – and are directly elected for a five-year period.

Because election procedures have not yet been unified in the member states, the elections are spread over a period of eight days. The French have a two-ballot system that calls for a seven-day interval between successive polls in constituencies where no single candidate has managed to obtain an absolute majority in the first round. The British never vote on a Sunday; others always do. In Belgium, voting is compulsory, unlike elsewhere.

There are no transnational voting lists or transnational political parties even though, in Parliament itself, one finds political groups that unite the MEPs with the same ideological attitudes (for example, Socialists, Christian Democrats, and Liberals) by caucuses and voting patterns. Most of these groups bear a party title and have indeed developed permanent organizations, but they are still a coalition of national parties with about the same label. The genuine European political parties that will probably one day emerge from this process will require truly European elections with European programs and lists, not an addition of 12 national elections with common themes, to be sure, but still dominated by national issues. In nearly every country, European elections are seen as tests for the government's majority. Commentators compare results not only with previous European elections but also with national and even local elections.

In most countries, MEPs are no longer members of their national parliaments, and the dual mandate, characteristic of the previous assembly, has been largely eliminated. Although this undoubtedly offers the advantage of eliminating potential conflicts of interests, it suffers the drawback of reducing the interest in Europe of some national parliaments to a level lower than when they delegated their own members to the assembly. These members used to keep their respective national parliaments informed and took part in national debates with European issues present in their minds.

To offset this absence of feedback from the activities of the European Parliament, a few national parliaments have set up special European committees in which both MEPs and their national colleagues take part.[14] These committees draw up reports that are then debated in the national parliament and serve as a means of controlling the government's European policies.

MEPs will sometimes be tempted to vote more along

national lines than European party lines. This may occur, though very seldom, when an issue is considered by all MEPs of any given country to be of major national interest. Even then, one will often encounter some minority dissenting opinions. European integration is at work here also. The rare national reaction will serve the useful purpose of letting others, as well as the Commission and the Council, know that a raw nerve has been rubbed.

The Parliament exercises its main powers in the complex and lengthy budgetary procedure where it shares responsibility for the annual EC budget with the Council of Ministers. Its legislative powers are nearly nonexistent, which explains the deep-seated frustration that appeared soon after the first direct elections. Disenchantment then set in among the newly elected members whose expectations had run high because of the substantial increase in political legitimacy flowing from a direct election. These expectations, however, directly clashed with the reality of the very limited powers of the assembly as laid out in the treaties. Many major figures thereupon left. A few remained, and the European Parliament set about the task of trying to enlarge its role, which it has so far managed to do only marginally. Although the latest treaty revisions provide for some cooperative decision making, the Parliament is far from satisfied.[15]

The treaties provide that Parliament give its advice before the Council of Ministers enacts legislation on the basis of a Commission proposal. But up to now, the Council has all too often taken only very limited notice of Parliament's opinion. This new "codecision" procedure ought to improve the situation somewhat; to what extent is not yet clear. Parliament has begun flexing its muscle, as will be discussed in chapter 7.

The Parliament in some ways supervises the activities of the Council of Ministers, through such parliamentary procedures as question time, special debates, resolutions, and specialized committees, in which ministers from the

Presidency take part. It also has the power to censure the Commission and to send it packing with a vote of no-confidence, but this has often been likened to the nuclear deterrent – good to have but never to use.[16] Asserting itself in this fashion really makes very little sense for the Parliament, because the Commission is an ally of Parliament in its permanent confrontation with the Council that keeps European integration lurching along its difficult path. In keeping with historical traditions, exemplified by the British Parliament's struggle against the powers of the sovereign, the MEPs have indeed concentrated their fire on the Council of Ministers. A majority of MEPs perceive the Council as embodying outdated nationalistic attitudes and low-common-denominator compromises that, although painstakingly devised, do not help Europe to integrate faster or become more efficient.

The Parliament was certainly instrumental in bringing about the latest revision of the treaty. Under the influence of one of its members, now deceased Italian ex-Communist Altiero Spinelli, it adopted a draft treaty with the object of creating a European Union. The European Parliament, devoid of any power to bring it into being, nonetheless struck a responsive chord in the public opinion of many member states. Governments were forced to react to the Parliament's controversial proposals. Those traditionally in favor of greater European integration welcomed it, while others felt compelled to forestall what they saw as premature, if not idealistic and therefore irrelevant, proposals. This led to the adoption of the Single European Act in 1987, which modified the treaties and provided for the "codecision" procedure.

That Parliament is frustrated is undeniable. MEPs are dissatisfied both with the role they can play as well as with the image they project to their electorates. All the polls show both a strong demand for "more Europe" in most member states and at the same time widespread discontent with EC institutions, and thus also with the Parliament. The next European elections will take place in June 1989. One can expect more tensions with the Council as MEPs grow increasingly worried that their limited powers will discourage a high voter turnout.

The European Court of Justice

Because of its limited relevance to the Presidency of the Council of Ministers, little will be said about the European Court of Justice. It has important powers, however, not only because it ensures that EC law is correctly implemented in the member states, but also because it interprets that law, thus promoting uniformity and playing a crucial role in furthering the integration process.[17] Many commentators have stressed this role and unhesitatingly present the court as the most efficient instrument for integration. The role is also largely recognized by the governments of the member states, as reflected in the latest treaty revisions in two significant ways.[18] First, new EC legislation provides for the possibility of a lower court to help reduce the present significant backlog of cases. Second, it now allows a member state specific and limited exceptions. Should either the Commission or a member state believe that a member state has abused this new possibility, they now have the right to refer directly to the Court of Justice, instead of following the far longer standard procedure.

Sitting in Luxembourg, the European Court of Justice is not to be confused with the European Court of Human Rights (in Strasbourg) or with the International Court of Justice (in The Hague), neither of which is an EC institution.

The Economic and Social Committee

A consultative body made up of representatives of the various sectors of economic activity in the 12 member states, the Economic and Social Committee (ESC) must, in the cases provided for by the treaties, be consulted before legislation can be enacted.[19] Its major utility lies in the opportunity it gives, through the forum it provides for trade unionists, professionals of all kinds, employers' associations, and consumer groups to meet and think on a European-wide level.

2

The General Affairs Council

The treaties that provided for the Council of Ministers merely stipulated that the governments of the member states should delegate one of its members to the Council without specifying which.[20] In the early stages of European integration, this one Council treated all EC matters, which was sufficient because the EC then had far fewer responsibilities. The Council was attended only by the foreign ministers, which might have seemed odd because it dealt with such matters as the production of coal and steel. In fact, these were sensitive and very political subjects then. The war had ended a mere six years before; Europe was still struggling to rebuild, and the Franco-German reconciliation was not evident. Questions about the EC were regarded as falling totally within the sphere of external relations.

At the time though, many were convinced that foreign ministers and diplomats would soon be ousted by specialists in financial and general economic matters. And that made sense for the early European federalists who saw the United States of Europe just around the corner. But that dream soon receded against the resilience of nationalism. International negotiating skills remained in high demand, while the specialists played major supporting roles.

Then came the discussions of the late 1950s and early 1960s about establishing a Common Agricultural Policy

(CAP). Foreign ministers had neither the expertise, time, nor endurance to sit through the marathon negotiations devoted to it. So they called in their agriculture colleagues for needed expertise, which started a trend that has blossomed into the present complex web of different council bodies. Although technically and legally equal, as will be explained later, this dazzling variety of councils can be classified into three different categories according to the frequency of their meetings and, more to the point, to their political weight.

In the first category is the General Affairs Council, also known as the Foreign Affairs Council. In the second are the ECOFIN Council, which deals with economic and financial matters, and the Agriculture Council. All the other councils form the third category. This does not mean that all meetings of the General Affairs Council are fundamental to the well-being of the EC, or that an Education Council will not make far-reaching decisions affecting the future of European universities. But for the purpose of explaining the functions of the council and the role of the Presidency, these three categories are the most convenient.

The General Affairs Council is attended by the foreign ministers, who meet every month except August.[21] It deals with the major policy issues of European integration in general, as well as with all foreign relations issues. It is also meant to coordinate the activities of the other councils, which it does, up to a point. It will continue to do so as long as it remains entrusted with its present responsibility for the preparation of the European Council, the semiannual meetings of the 12 prime ministers together with the French president (see Chapter 6). Let us consider these various elements in succession.

Composition and Role

Foreign ministers attend the General Affairs Council according to a tradition established at the EC's inception. The Council's name, a fairly recent one, used to be the Foreign

Affairs Council because of its membership, not because of the subjects it dealt with. The proliferation of specialized councils had created the need for a coordination role, and the European Council, as will be apparent later, was not the answer. Since 1957 foreign ministries had developed considerable expertise in dealing with European integration in general. Within governments, foreign ministers had been entrusted with the responsibility for overall European policy for so long that no one saw any need for a change. Certainly, some of their specialized colleagues and their civil servants would be far more knowledgeable in their relevant sector of expertise, but none of them had an overall view, nor were their staff trained for this. In addition, foreign ministries had the experience of coordinating various national departments before undertaking international negotiations. So the practice continued from the early day of the EC to the present, not without resistance and resentment from other ministries.

Two factors played an important role in bolstering the relevance of the General Affairs Council. First, the Commission shared with the foreign ministries a need for at least one council that cultivated a sense of the overall complexity of the integration process – a forum in which specialized national interests were kept in greater perspective than in the other councils. This was found in the General Affairs Council. The Commission thus used its privilege of introducing legislation but also of deciding which members of the Commission to send to which council and where to make important announcements to enhance subtly the role of this Council. Second, because it prepares the European Council – and the foreign minister is the only minister to sit there next to his prime minister – the General Affairs Council has maintained a certain political preeminence.

Most foreign ministers are nowadays supported by a junior minister who substitutes for the minister during part of the meeting or even for the whole of it.[22] If internal political crisis or transportation problems prevent the ministerial team from reaching Brussels or Luxembourg before the

Council starts, the permanent representative replaces his absent minister.

Meetings are usually held once a month, spanning a Monday and a Tuesday. According to the agenda, they start on Monday morning or with lunch that day, a difference that matters to the Greeks, Italians, and Portuguese; they either must reach Brussels on Sunday evening for an early Monday start or must leave their capitals on Monday morning to be on time for lunch. All meetings are held in Brussels, except during the months of April, June, and October. In those three months, they take place in Luxembourg, which reflects this city's strong desire to remain in the running for the role of capital of Europe as well as the compromises reached when the European Coal and Steel Community moved to Brussels from its initial base in Luxembourg. This is a typical example of the need for compromise to sometimes overrule mere logic, because Luxembourg is, indeed, an inconvenient place to meet. Air links with the rest of Europe are few. A massive migration of staff and documents takes place from Brussels, home of the Council Secretariat, of the Commission, and of the member states' permanent missions. Although everyone puts up more or less cheerfully with the inconvenience, it is clear to all that this situation cannot last indefinitely.

Preparation

To prepare for any meeting of the Council, the Presidency, which is in charge of running it, will have had contacts with the Commission. The format varies from one Presidency to another, but basically the same pattern is followed. The foreign minister is briefed in great detail by both his permanent representative and the general secretary of the Council. They essentially report to him the state of discussions in COREPER and the reasons why this subject appears on the agenda, the positions taken by the member states in response to the Commission's proposal, and their estimate as to what the Presidency might to able to achieve. The objectives vary. The Council might want to comment on a Commission report on difficult trade negotiations and give it political support. The Presidency might think it useful to start putting up an issue for initial consideration by ministers with a view to a decision in a subsequent meeting. Or it might decide that the time has come to push an issue to the decision stage.

Both the permanent representative and the general secretary give the minister their advice on the more promising course of action to achieve results. Sometimes the briefings go into great technical detail because of the complexity of the matter and its sensitivity for one or several member states. In really difficult cases, the minister consults with one or several of his colleagues beforehand either to firm up a majority, to get a better personal insight into some of his colleagues' problems, or simply to apply pressure when he thinks it is needed.

To help him in his task, the president receives an excellent briefing book with comments and suggestions from the Council Secretariat, which is seen beforehand by the permanent representative or drawn up in cooperation with him or with one of his senior assistants. Everything a president might need is there – the status of every issue pending before the Council is described, as well as its background. Recommended alternative tactics are explained. When required, language is also provided to help the president navigate skillfully through the shoals of national sensitivities by uttering just the right words. These documents, which are for the president only, are a first-class instrument, much appreciated by any Presidency, and their loss is much regretted once the Presidency is over. The minister or the president of COREPER will now and then show the relevant pages to a colleague to confirm that the scenario, as laid out, will indeed help overcome that particular delegation's remaining problems.

Before the meeting, the president of the Council also

sits down with the Commission. Each is accompanied by a limited number of aides. On the Presidency side, the permanent representative and the general secretary of the Council are present, as a general rule. Depending upon the subject, the minister will talk to the president of the Commission, to a more directly concerned member of the Commission, or to several members. This meeting is essential because of the Commission's special powers and its unique role in introducing legislation, but, more to the point, because it is able to modify its proposals as the discussion goes on in the Council. Efficient presidencies, as a general rule, are those that have maintained a close and confident working relationship with the Commission. These meetings are much shorter than the briefings, because the facts are well known and most of the time the tactics have been worked out in advance by the permanent representative and the Council Secretariat with the Commission's representative in COREPER.

Running the Meeting: The Issue of Voting

Because of national political requirements and sensitivities, fairly elaborate scenarios sometimes have to be drawn up — for example, the case of a lone dissenting member state on a matter requiring unanimity. Discussions in COREPER will have made it abundantly clear that the dissenter is isolated, with no hope of further changing the Commission's proposal to accommodate the more obvious problems. A strong national lobby prevents a weak government from changing its stance, even though it has gradually become convinced either that it cannot indefinitely block this legislation or even that it might not be such a bad thing after all if it were adopted. That country's permanent representative has many direct or indirect ways of explaining to his colleague in the president's chair that his instructions might change, but not straightaway because of a strong lobby back home. The Presidency will then probably put that subject on the agenda to give the beleaguered minister the opportunity for a spirited presentation of his case, which will be played back in full in his country's media. At the same time, that particular delegation's total isolation will be made glaringly evident. At the next Council meeting this scenario may be repeated, so that the first remarks can be made about the need also to take the larger European requirements into account while, of course, never neglecting national concerns. Many arguments – for example, duress, the pressure of the other member states, and a sense of the greater European good – are available to resourceful politicians to help them explain why they were compelled to give up a position so stoutly defended.

This scenario, although imaginary, is pretty close to what often happens. It helps show how crucial it is for the Presidency to be well informed and subtle in its running of the Council. In effect, this is a permanent negotiating forum, with 13 players each having different concerns and different political weight.

Fortunately, it is not always so difficult to make a decision. To begin with, there is a whole range of decisions that are merely rubber-stamped by a Council that will not even have considered them. Agreements in these cases have been reached in COREPER and are formally adopted by the Council because this is required to give them legal existence. Known as the "A" items, they are usually handled at the start of the meeting. Some very important decisions are made in this fashion, and the Presidency will have to make certain that the press does not overlook the more significant ones. Some delegations prefer to see a decision as a specific agenda item because they attach a special importance to it and feel that the "A"-item procedure does not underline this sufficiently. Other decisions are easily made by the Council without a great deal of discussion. And in some cases, a discussion does take place, but voting is provided for by the treaties, which helps to expedite matters.

The issue of voting has long been a major handicap to

efficient decision making. Ever since the Luxembourg Compromise of 1966, voting has seldom taken place, even when the treaties clearly provided for it.[23] France's policy of trying to defer any vote until consensus – that is, unanimity – had been achieved on what France termed an important national issue was bolstered by the new EC members. Refusing to vote was unnecessary. A delegation could merely declare that an important national interest was at stake, and the Presidency was effectively denied the voting option. Indecision, as such, could not realistically be challenged before the Court of Justice. And even when that option might have been legally promising, on political grounds it never was. Everyone knew that, given the opportunity, the court might well state that the treaty provisions had to be respected, thus killing the Luxembourg Compromise. No member state dared haul another one before the court on this issue.

Some who were ostensibly hostile to the Luxembourg Compromise were in fact happy with its continued existence as a reassurance against unforeseen conditions. The German minister of agriculture even invoked it once recently, though he was roundly criticized for doing so, and Germany quickly proclaimed that it would never happen again. The Commission also did not want to run the risk of confronting the offending member states. Retaliation possibilities against another member state or against the Commission were simply too numerous to be ignored.

Matters began to change, however, with the prospect of the Spanish and Portuguese accessions. A 12-member EC was seen by all as courting permanent paralysis. And so, gradually, voting crept back into EC practice. The turning point is held by some to have come in 1982, when the Presidency at that time, confronted with a British veto that would have meant no decision on the annual agricultural prices, decided to go ahead and call for a vote anyway.[24] The Presidency cleverly refrained from raising the procedural issue, because it would have put some member states in a

difficult position on a matter of principle. It also knew that
the other member states most likely to oppose taking a vote
when someone invoked a national interest were this time
vitally interested in seeing timely decisions.

The British delegation found itself in a minority. The
decision taken by the Council was legally unimpeachable
and, although doing so with bad grace, the British minister
of agriculture was forced to comply with it. A modest, but
significant, psychological breakthrough was achieved,
which led all succeeding presidencies, including the French
and the British, to call more and more often for a vote. It
also laid the groundwork for the 1985 treaty revisions that
provide for greater use of the vote. As a result, the Presidency has acquired a much greater freedom of action. It will
hardly ever issue surprise vote calls. Rather, it will try to
wear down opposition and build as much of a consensus
before using this possibility, all the time quietly reminding
everyone of its availability. Every delegation will thus negotiate accordingly and try to achieve some improvements on
the proposed legislation before a vote makes it definitive.
Subtlety, good negotiating skills, and a thorough knowledge of the issues and of their triple (national, EC, and international) impact are thus required to be successful in this
demanding and complex environment.

The meeting itself lasts up to two days—obviously the
duration varies with the agenda. Unless special events have
taken place, Council meetings tend to be short—a day or
less—in the early months of the Presidency and grow longer
as the Presidency moves toward the end of its term and the
meeting of the European Council.

Meals are an important ingredient. Indeed, the Presidency circulates beforehand a list of items to be raised during the lunch by the participants. The Presidency and the
Commission usually list the greater number of items, because the lunchtime discussion provides for good informal
sounding on more delicate matters. But it is by no means
rare to see another minister announce beforehand that he or

she will want to raise a few specific issues. Also, a dead-locked discussion in the formal meeting of the Council can sometimes become unstuck in the more relaxed luncheon atmosphere with its greater possibilities for ministerial candor.

Apart from the ministers and one member of the Commission, only the permanent representative of the Presidency, the general secretary of the Council, and one senior civil servant from the Commission are allowed to sit at the table. They will ensure that a proper but informal record of the discussion is made available to all of their colleagues. Some ministers do brief their delegations very well after lunch. Others are less consistent. Because the Council itself or COREPER usually have to follow up, it is very important to make sure that everyone is fully aware of the course of the discussion and, above all, of the decisions made during these lunches that will have to be formalized afterward.

A Typical Agenda

Consider the following typical agenda for a General Affairs Council meeting held in the final month of a Presidency that covered the first six months of the year.

1. *Consideration of European Parliament resolutions.* Traditionally first on the agenda, this item usually is dealt with in a few minutes because of the number and the general irrelevance of most of these resolutions, which are an expression of "the sense of the European Parliament." Given Parliament's sensitivity with this superficial handling by the Council, the Presidency has taken the habit of drawing the attention of the member states to some of the more significant resolutions. But this is mere window dressing, because no one gives them much thought. The new provisions of the Single European Act are likely to change this and to bolster Parliament's influence.

2. *Adoption of the "A" items.* In this procedure, which

was discussed earlier, delegations know beforehand what to expect, because agreement has been reached in COREPER. Every now and then a delegation asks for a delay because of some last-minute problem and then gives the final go-ahead later in the course of the meeting. If it cannot do so then, the contentious item is removed from the list and reintroduced at the next Council meeting.

3. *Trade relations with the United States and Japan.* This topic is an example of the first item of substance to be handled. The discussion will usually begin with a status report by the commissioner in charge. Foreign ministers might be joined by their trade colleagues and, if the issues are sensitive or if the discussion requires confidentiality, a restricted session might be called. In most cases, the Commission will be requesting political support from the Council for the negotiations that are almost permanently under way (for example, the Airbus and agriculture discussions with the United States or market access for European products in Japan). In some instances it will ask for a fresh mandate or for a change in the existing mandate. Discussion will often be complicated by the differing interests of the delegations — for example, the case of U.S. wheat imports to Spain. Spain wanted to keep the imports at existing cheaper levels, at least during the transitional period before full application of the CAP, while EC grain producers wanted to benefit as soon as possible from the Community preference as a result of Spanish accession. In such a case, both Commission and Presidency will have to help in actively establishing a compromise solution.

4. *The setting of maximum acceptable levels for foodstuff radiation.* As a consequence of the Chernobyl accident, measurements were taken in all member states to forbid the import of foodstuffs from countries where radiation levels were thought to be high. Some regions of the EC had been affected, and there was considerable disagreement among experts as to the radiation levels that could be tolerated in milk, fruit, and vegetables. Political conditions in the member states surfaced in the debate; countries with

active ecology parties were more inclined to be restrictive than others. The risks of reintroducing barriers to trade were high. Media attention was great. This kind of tricky scenario has a high emotional charge that can lead to a long and frustrating debate and taxes the skills of any Presidency. The Council did take many months before coming to any agreement on this issue.

5. *Discussion of EC relations with an associate country, such as Morocco, Israel, or Cyprus.* The EC has established an extensive network of agreements with a great number of Third World countries. Special emphasis has been put on those bordering the Mediterranean and on the African, Caribbean, and Pacific (ACP) countries. Joint Council sessions are held with these countries or groups. They are usually held right after a meeting of the General Affairs Council. In most cases, the discussion will be short because the preparatory work will have led to a prearranged scenario and to conclusions agreed upon beforehand. But sometimes ministers have to resolve a problem at their political level. And both the Presidency and the Commission want to be certain that their statements will correctly reflect the common position, because they alone will be taking the floor on behalf of the EC. Before the joint meeting, they hold an informal discussion with the minister leading the other delegation, either to make sure that the prearranged scenario is acceptable or to iron out last-minute differences. Because this is not always fully in order, a parallel negotiation takes place at the senior civil servant level while the General Affairs Council meeting is in progress. The Presidency team will be under a lot of pressure during this two-ring circus act.

6. *Preparation for the European Council.* This agenda item is not always as important as it appears to be. Rarely do substantial discussions take place at this stage before the European Council. Most of the other specialized council meetings have already taken place, and every delegation knows what their outcome has been. The General Affairs Council will have dealt with the substantive issues that concern it directly. The Commission, to preserve its cher-

ished freedom of action, will not yet have issued the papers that will form the basis for some of the prime ministers' discussions.

Recently the tendency has been to hold a special meeting of the foreign ministers during the preceding weekend specifically devoted to one or two of the more important issues facing the government leaders. This practice grew out of the complex discussions that led to the Single European Act in 1986, when a preliminary high-level meeting was needed to identify the most sensitive political issues, to prepare the ground to be covered by the prime ministers, to force national governments to address the main problems before the European Council, and to start making the inevitable internal compromises between the conflicting national interests. Experience has indeed shown that insufficiently prepared leaders find it very difficult to solve problems unfamiliar to them.

But at this late stage, the General Affairs Council will usually content itself with a review of all the issues on the European Council's agenda. This enables the Presidency to carry out a last check of where delegations stand on some of the more intractable issues and gives delegations a first indication of the probable scenario for the European Council meeting.

This last meeting also allows the General Affairs Council to play its coordinating role and to bring together the conclusions reached by the specialized councils. At this stage the Council sometimes decides that the European Council is faced with too many issues or that some of them are not ripe for consideration. The Council treads cautiously here. It is not always easy for a foreign minister to risk the wrath of another cabinet colleague not glad to see a favored issue wiped from the European Council's agenda. As always, some colleagues are more equal than others, and their respective weights inside their governments will be felt more or less strongly. The conclusions reached by finance or agriculture ministers will nearly always be passed on to the prime ministers. The same is not as true for transport or environment ministers, whatever the relevance of the issues brought forward by their council.

7. *Preparation for the next Economic Summit.*[25] Although placement in this list does not necessarily indicate its order of occurrence, this agenda item will be discussed here to illustrate the workings of the council. Western Economic Summits, usually held every spring, are an established feature of international life. Seven participants are mentioned in most dispatches, but there are in fact eight. The list of Canada, West Germany, France, Italy, Japan, the United Kingdom, and the United States must indeed include the EC. The EC has been represented by both the Presidency and the Commission ever since the London Summit of 1977, which Roy Jenkins was the first to attend in his capacity as president of the Commission.

Because the summits became institutionalized, the Commission and the smaller member states had protested that issues of exclusive Community competence, such as trade, were being discussed in the absence of the EC. This was reluctantly conceded by some of the European participants and initially resisted by the United States, which eventually gave way under European pressure. To some of the major European states, the presence of the EC came as an unwelcome reminder of their diminished importance on the world economic scene. Others were in favor of it. The Americans, but also the Japanese, did not want yet another European around a table where they already saw too many of them.

Until the latest enlargement of the EC, the Economic Summits could always be scheduled to avoid the presence of a smaller member state holding the Presidency. The sole exception to this well-enforced rule was the 1982 Versailles Summit, scheduled during the Belgian Presidency. Belgian Prime Minister Wilfried Martens and Foreign Minister Léo Tindemans attended together with Commission President Gaston Thorn. But this was very much viewed as an exception, not soon to be repeated. With 12 member states, however, it became impossible to continue this restrictive practice. The Dutch Presidency attended the 1986 Tokyo Summit, and the Belgian ministers present in Versailles turned up in Venice the following year.

The smaller member states have tried using their Presidency to force the EC to adopt common positions ahead of the summit meetings, which, not surprisingly, has not elicited a very enthusiastic response from the larger member states. The Commission itself has been ambiguous about this, because it has known that common positions would be difficult to reach. Feeling merely tolerated at these summits, it did not want to be seen as encouraging the full emergence of another European player around the table. This it believed to be desirable in the long term, but premature as long as the EC is not fully integrated and capable of speaking authoritatively with a single voice. On the other hand, it wanted to be seen as defending the interest of the EC as a whole, this being its raison d'être and the justification for its tolerated presence at the summits.

So the General Affairs Council has followed the practice of putting this item on its agenda. Ministers from the nonparticipant countries make comments after having heard a presentation by the Commission "sherpa" – the pretentious nickname given to the senior aide in charge of smoothing his leader's ascent to the summit. "Sherpas" jointly prepare documents that are submitted to the leaders. In the case of the EC, these papers are in the hands of the Presidency and the Commission, who elect either to show them to the other member states or to make a resumé available for discussion in the Council. Sometimes the leaders do make use of these papers. Often disregarded by them, they nonetheless serve two useful purposes. First, they identify the issues, thus giving people an opportunity to concentrate on them. And, second, they afford leaders a welcome chance to demonstrate their independence of their sherpas.

So far, the successive presidencies have not been very successful in attempting to reach common and binding positions. To begin with, subjects relating to foreign policy

and terrorism, as well as monetary matters, still fall outside
EC competence. And although a rundown of the main summit issues shows clearly that the majority are legitimate
subjects for debate within the EC, it is not likely that the
present European participants will agree in the near future
to formalize common positions in advance of summit meetings.[26] Doing so would expose them to the risk of U.S. and
Japanese questions on the continued need for so many Europeans at the summits. And no present European leader is
likely to abandon soon the prestige deriving from summit
participation.

Package Deals

The Presidency also often makes use of a special technique
to hasten the adoption of decisions long stranded by the
opposition of a single member state. The technique is used
especially for harmonizing legislation or removing technical
barriers to trade. The Presidency sets up a package deal of
carefully selected items. The sum total is attractive to all
member states, but the price to be paid by each is the approval of one or two directives that have long been resisted.
When the Presidency, with the help of the Commission,
skillfully wheels and deals, this technique is efficient and
usually yields the desired result. Because it requires a sufficient backlog of pending decisions before it can successfully
be used, this technique is available only once or twice to
each Presidency and sometimes less than that, especially if
the previous Presidency made use of it just before the end of
its term of office.

Plenary or Restricted Sessions?

The General Affairs Council meets in different formats, but
the most common is the plenary session. Each delegation
has six or eight seats, depending on the size of the meeting

room. The Commission and the Presidency are allowed double that number. One interesting feature worth noting is that the Presidency team is divided in two different delegations. One sits at the head of the large rectangular table, opposite the Commission, with all the delegations seated on the remaining two sides of the table. The presiding minister is flanked on his right by his permanent representative and a few aides. On his left sits the general secretary of the Council, a legal adviser, and secretariat staff. The other part of the Presidency delegation sits as a national delegation, behind the panel bearing the name of the country.

This arrangement, devised to enable the Presidency to function without the constraints of simultaneously defending national positions, works differently according to the countries holding the presidency. The entrenched integrationists play the game fairly honestly, and their national delegation rarely intervenes. There are two main reasons for doing so—either needing to cast a vote or having to defend a position at odds with a proposed presidential compromise; both rarely occur. Others use their presidential period to promote national interests more or less blatantly. This is not always a bad thing; some national interests coincide with the overall interests of the majority. But when this pursuit becomes too obvious, reactions from the Commission or the other member states can be expected, with negative results for all, as will be apparent in later chapters.

The plenary session is not ideal for promoting discretion. About 130 persons are present in the room, along with the interpreters and the technical staff. The Presidency therefore frequently uses several kinds of restricted sessions—the most restricted for ministers only, along with the Presidency's permanent representative and the general secretary. The most common such session limits delegations to the people sitting at the main table, three to four per delegation. As explained earlier, meals are also useful for discretionary purposes.

Languages: A Major Headache

The Presidency also must worry about languages. There are nine official languages in the Community, and Council meetings are held in all nine.[27] Although obviously burdensome and not conducive to maximum efficiency, this is a necessary constraint of the integration process. Many Council decisions are legally binding in all member states. They simply have to be available in every country's national idiom. On top of that, ministers are not always fluent in all languages of the EC, even though most of them manage to get along very well in English, French, or German. Because they cannot be expected to agree to being at a disadvantage to their colleagues, simultaneous translation of the highest quality is provided by a large and expert team of translators and interpreters. Many believe them to be the best in the world, and they do perform extremely well under difficult and tiring conditions. Some have become so expert that they can translate the sense of a joke and make Danes laugh at a pun pronounced in Greek. They are present in all the meetings, even the most restricted ones – in fact, everywhere translation is required, which includes one-on-one meetings between delegation heads on some very sensitive issues. This multiplicity of languages often gives rise to misunderstandings, despite the quality of the interpreters, and the Presidency must be constantly on the alert for such a problem, which can mar the smooth flow of a debate and block the Council's activity.

The frequent use of written amendments during a debate further complicates the president's job. When the Commission or the Presidency wishes to do so, they have normally had the time to prepare versions in all languages. But this is seldom the case when the amendment is introduced by another delegation. Long delays can ensue, and the president will try to avoid this by going on to another agenda item and coming back to the first one when all translations are available. In some fortunate cases, delegations will agree to work with only English and French texts, but final agreement will be conditional on the availability of the document in all national languages.

Press Relations

At the end of every Council meeting, the president holds a press conference, usually together with the Commission member on hand for the meeting. He will summarize the Council discussions, stressing the achievements, pointing to some decisions taken under the "A"-item procedure, and avoiding too many details about disagreements in order not to jeopardize his chances of reaching a compromise in a future meeting. But the press is very well informed of even the more restricted discussions. National spokesmen have all through the meeting been busy feeding their national press with details of the positions taken by their minister and his opponents. Other journalists will have heard this too. Documents have a habit of falling rapidly into the hands of the press, sometimes even before delegations have seen them. In spite of all the efforts of the Presidency and the Council Secretariat to prevent this from happening, there are often too many interested parties, and leaks are too tempting.

At his press conference, the president will be confronted by a large multinational press corps, attendance obviously fluctuating in relation to the subjects discussed. For the more multilingual of them, interviews in several languages follow. Ministers will also use the press conference to pressure some of their colleagues and so prepare the ground for the next meeting. The president is not supposed to reveal the identity of dissenting ministers, but that is asking a lot of a politician who has had to steer a difficult meeting and is often tired, nervous, and frustrated by the ambiguous outcome of a Council meeting for which he has painstakingly prepared.

3

The Other Councils

There are two other categories of councils besides the first – that is, the General Affairs Council. The second includes the ECOFIN and Agriculture councils; the third includes all the remaining ones. The preparation and running of the meetings, the voting, and the language problems apply equally to all three.

The ECOFIN Council

ECOFIN regroups the finance ministers, sometimes accompanied by their colleagues in charge of economic matters. They are usually flanked by a junior minister, much like their foreign affairs counterparts. They also meet monthly and have informal weekend meetings at least once every six months. COREPER prepares their meetings and supervises many working groups specializing in matters dealt with by ECOFIN. An exception is the Monetary Committee, in which senior civil servants from the finance ministries keep a close eye on the running of the European Monetary System (EMS) and advise their ministers without referring to COREPER. Monetary matters are considered too sensitive to be handled by anyone but a close-knit, discrete group of experts with direct access to their ministers.

ECOFIN deals mostly with the EMS, the economic situation of the EC, financial and customs regulations, export credit policy, and the frame of reference for the EC's annual budget. It also considers the financial and economic implications of the major issues facing the EC. Finance ministers thus give their opinion on the accession of candidate countries and on Commission proposals to implement the Single European Act. They also prepare the European Council's reflections on the economic and financial state of the EC. Their document is then supposedly considered by the General Affairs Council when it puts the finishing touches to the overall preparation of the European Council. In practice, ECOFIN is purposefully scheduled so close to the European Council that it becomes very difficult for the foreign ministers to do anything but pass the document on to the prime ministers.

One of the main tasks of the ECOFIN council is its responsibility for the EMS, the embryo of a fully developed currency with a single controlling authority. Given the obvious political implications of such a step, it has stagnated at its first stage. Former French Prime Minister Valéry Giscard d'Estaing and German Chancellor Helmut Schmidt initiated it at the July 1978 European Council in Bremen and at the meeting in Brussels on December 4 and 5 of that year. They secured the agreement of all the participants to the establishment of a system based on a common monetary unit, the European Currency Unit (ECU), which was primarily designed to give the European currency exchange rates greater stability in periods of major currency swings.[28] Preferential credit was made available to the central banks on a standby basis to bolster this mechanism. The founders clearly intended to move beyond that stage and to establish a European Monetary Fund two years after the EMS was created, with the proviso that a much greater degree of convergence had to be reached on the economic policies of the member states for this system to become successful. The required unanimity could not be found to reach that second stage. The German Bundesbank reacted to what it considered an inacceptable fait accompli on the part of Chancellor Schmidt. In addition, economic conditions within the EC were not at the time conducive to further advances in European monetary integration. Several countries pursued economic policies too far apart from those of the others, the main example of this being the policies of the French Socialist government in 1981. The British never fully took part, the Italians benefited from special exchange rate margins, the Belgians maintained their system of dual exchange rates, and the new members' currencies were not part of the system.

In view of all these negative elements, the success of the ECU caught central bankers and government leaders by surprise. More and more economic operators within Europe—especially in the weaker currency countries because of the greater exchange security—began using the ECU. Luxembourg set up a modest but growing ECU bond market. And the European central banks saw merit in the increased stability between their currencies as a result of the EMS. Some forward movement is again apparent now that agreement has been reached on the goal of a single unified market by the end of 1992. Such a market will require a common currency if capital and services are to move really freely inside it.

One spectacular aspect of the finance ministers' responsibility for the EMS has been their last-minute weekend meetings to realign exchange rates when this became necessary. Monetary matters are still so laden with the emotional symbolism of national sovereignty that some of these meetings have taken a fairly dramatic turn. Finance ministers do not like giving their electors the impression that other member states have managed their economy better and that they have to adjust accordingly. Everyone then plays the game differently. The strong currency countries—mostly Germany and the Netherlands—try to avoid having to revalue or, if this is unavoidable, try to revalue as little as possible.

The middle range of countries pursue different strategies depending on their immediate goals. Some of them are happy with a symbolic revaluation, say 1 or 2 percent, which compares them favorably with their constituents and, more important, with the world financial community. Others adamantly oppose any movement up or down to give an impression of great stability when others fluctuate. And if devaluation is necessary, they seek to keep it as small as possible in the hope that someone else's greater devaluation will cast them in a favorable light. Finally, the weaker currency countries might try to devalue more than their economic situation would justify for competitive reasons. What are in general fairly minor adjustments can sometimes, as a result, be blown out of proportion.

The Agriculture Council

The other important council in the second category is the Agriculture Council. Its importance stems from the unbalanced weight given to the CAP in the EC. As much as 75 percent of the EC budget has on occasion been devoted to agricultural expenses. This unhealthy situation reflects the EC's incapacity to move significantly toward other policies after the early deals were struck establishing the CAP. Over the years powerful farm lobbies have effectively protected farmers, mostly large ones, against unwanted reforms. Agriculture ministers have had no incentives to make great efforts at changing the situation and have run obvious political risks in attempting to do so. The remaining government members might have been more mindful of the overall economic picture, especially the finance or budget ministers, but the farm lobbies usually managed to elicit sufficient political support to quash any attempt at reform.

Things started changing with British membership in the EC. The structure of British agriculture was quite different from that of the other member states. The British were more interested in seeing other policies developed, because they did not benefit as much as the others from existing financial transfers in favor of farmers. Because the funds simply were not available to do this, a debate started about the size of the British contribution to the EC budget, which culminated in the 1982 Fontainebleau agreement that gave the British a rebate on their budget contribution.

At the same time, it became obvious that the EC could no longer afford its policy of price guarantees to producers that resulted in massive overproduction, spiraling storage costs, disruptions in the world agriculture markets, and the consequent difficult relations with the other major producers and most developing countries. The perspective of the upcoming Uruguay GATT Round came as an added impetus. Agriculture ministers were well aware of this and started taking corrective measures. The process has developed quite substantially, and the EC is now well on its way toward controlling and eventually reducing the cost of its agricultural policy, as it did, for example, in the February 1988 European Council.[29]

The preceding discussion illustrates the importance of this council. Some of its topics are so technical that it evolved a special structure to deal with them – the Special Agricultural Committee. It substitutes for COREPER and also sits at the top of many working groups reporting directly to it. Because of the financial and political implications of many of the Agriculture Council's decisions, however, COREPER does handle the more politically sensitive issues. Finance and foreign ministers also debate them, sometimes to the displeasure of their agriculture colleagues who resent the impression of being held under control by others. As recent EC history amply demonstrates, however, that control has been largely symbolic, and agriculture ministers have managed to have things pretty much as they want them.

Although this volume cannot analyze the workings of this council in any depth, it is interesting to note some of the more significant issues dealt with over a period of six months – that is, January to July 1987. The council successively discussed such matters as the impact of one of the recurring monetary adjustments on the price support mechanism; the possibility of using existing stocks to alleviate the plight of people suffering from a cold wave over Europe; adjustments to the beef, dairy, and wine-growing sectors with a view to reducing intervention costs; structural measures to help the smaller farmers; the establishment of agricultural prices for the next crop year; and veterinary problems. Of all these subjects, by far the most important is the establishment of agricultural prices for the following campaign, because the income of nearly all European farmers depends upon the decisions taken in Brussels. The Commission proposals are carefully reviewed and criticized by the various farmer unions, and great publicity is given by the press to their reactions. Ministers are intensively lobbied. The Agricultural Council devotes several formal sessions and at least one informal session to discussing this point. Although not having much say in this debate, the European Parliament follows it closely. Farmers take part in European elections, and their well-organized lobbies make sure that their members recall the positions taken by MEPs on these matters.

The Other Specialized Councils

The third category comprises the many other councils. None of them meets as frequently as those that have been mentioned up to now. Some are quite important in their own right, and nearly all make significant decisions at one time or another. The proliferation of different councils reflects the growing complexity of European integration as well as the desire of most so-called technical ministers to get a piece of the European action, which is seen as steadily more relevant to any government responsibility. The general directorates of the Commission are not altogether blameless either in this development. Most of them also believe that more can and must be done in their particular field. They accordingly propose new legislation, which is gladly accepted by some underemployed members of an oversized Commission who are not content just to be part of the team and want to play a significant role.

As European policies developed over the years, new councils came into being. At present, there are councils dealing with industry, research and development, budget, internal market, environment, development aid, transport, fisheries, and social affairs; these are well established and deal with areas of undisputed EC competence. Still other councils meet on matters that are not as clearly within their competence, while ministers from the member countries believe they have to get together at regular intervals to coordinate them, or at least compare their national policies concerning them. Legally speaking, some of these meetings are not council meetings as such – a distinction not directly relevant to the purpose of examining how a Presidency functions since the same preparation and running of these meetings are involved.

The budget ministers meet in the second half of the year to establish the *annual EC budget* according to a set procedure, with established time constraints and a specific role for the European Parliament, which shares this responsibility with the Council. As a result, negotiations with the Parliament take place every year. In the recent past, they have been difficult because of the perennial EC budget crisis brought on by the unwillingness of some member states to increase the budget as long as agriculture costs are not brought under control. Parliament must formally adopt the budget and has refused to do so several times because of insufficient funding, thus forcing the EC to start its fiscal year with "provisional twelfths." This means that it is only allowed to spend as much as it did the previous year and only for existing policies, not for new ones. This has effectively forced reluctant governments into grudgingly providing the necessary funds, with considerable political costs to the EC, especially in terms of its image with public opinion. The February 1988 European Council settled this issue for some years to come, so this will not be a problem in the near future.[30]

Fisheries are governed by an established common policy, and negotiations occur every year to allocate limited stocks to the fishermen of the EC, both in waters of EC countries and in those of countries with which it has concluded agreements. This council thus plays both an internal and an international role. The foreign ministers do not intervene as long as things remain simple and negotiations with third countries focus only on fishery matters. In practice, however, matters are often more complex, usually because other politically sensitive issues are involved. The General Affairs Council then steps in and tries to solve the political problem before sending the issue back to the fisheries ministers.

Another major area of interest is that of the *internal market* that the EC proposes to establish by the end of 1992. The title Internal Market Council misleadingly implies overall responsibility for the establishment of the internal market, whereas this council actually deals with parts of it. But some of them are very important – for example, mutual recognition of degrees, border controls, patents, and a host of more technical but economically significant measures. Both the ECOFIN and the Agriculture councils also make important decisions affecting the internal market.

The EC has a large *foreign aid program* overseen by the Development Aid Council, which meets once or twice a year. The other new councils follow a similar pattern. COREPER is responsible for the preparation of every single council session and, in theory at least, the General Affairs Council has to be appraised of the results of these meetings. Because this is impossible in practice, foreign ministers are content with information given by their permanent representatives, whose duties require constant attention to the coherence of policies defended in the multiple council meetings by different ministers with different sets of priorities. All the working groups report to COREPER – with the few exceptions mentioned earlier – and the permanent representatives then decide whether or not an issue is ripe for consideration by the ministers.

In some instances, there also is a discussion as to which council will handle a given subject, and permanent representatives may have to reconcile different viewpoints among their ministers on this issue as well. The Commission also plays a role and expresses its preference on the forum. Some pulling and shoving takes place inside the Commission because some commissioners prefer a particular presiding minister or a more sympathetic forum, be it a specialized council or the foreign ministers. And the Presidency must reconcile all of these different aspirations because it has the final word on the decision to send any issue on to a particular council meeting. The better presidencies will use this power with prudence but also with determination if necessary, avoiding hasty decisions that often lead to stalemate but taking the lead in the case of prolonged irresolution.

Every one of these council meetings is technically and legally equal. All are considered as *the* council. Legislation adopted in one of them is as valid as that adopted in any other. This is a useful feature since it enables the Presidency to use the "A"-items procedure to get, for example, an ECOFIN council meeting to adopt a decision without having to wait for the next meeting of the relevant council, which could very well be several months later. Once again it is the job of COREPER to make certain that the proposed list of "A" items for any council meeting is correct. As stated above, though, the General Affairs Council is in political terms slightly more equal than the others.

The Role of the Presidency

The existence of so many council meetings reveals quite a lot about the extent of European integration. It also means that the machinery has become complex, cumbersome, and difficult to coordinate. And that, of course, is precisely where the Presidency comes in. Its main responsibility is to ensure that the necessary coordination takes place, which in turn means that nearly the whole government of the presiding member state is fully involved in the Presidency at all levels – ministerial as well as administrative. As has become apparent, COREPER plays a major role in deciding which proposals are ripe for council consideration and by which council. An active Presidency will lean very heavily on the ambassador presiding over COREPER, thus making him a key player. COREPER is the place where political sensitivities as well as major economic or technical difficulties will be signaled by member states ahead of council meetings. The Presidency will then have the choice to push the issue, keep the debate at the COREPER level, or refer it to the working group for further consideration.

Every Presidency makes considerable effort to negotiate with the other member states, with the Commission, and often with its national authorities. A better school for negotiating skills is hard to find, which is why all member states go to great pains to get their best bureaucrats into European affairs. Some member states, especially those holding the Presidency for the first time, use their Presidency to reorganize their government and make their EC participation more effective. When the issues at stake involve an external partner, an extra layer of negotiations is merely added.

The personal determination of the minister presiding over the Council often makes a difference, provided the necessary elements are all there. Stamina, staying power, and a solid grasp of the issues, as well as political sensitivity or "fingerspitzgefühl" are essential requirements for this very demanding task. Over the years, long-serving ministers and their officials get to know each other well. Strengths and weaknesses cannot remain hidden. And these elements will also enter into the calculations of a Presidency weighing its options before a Council meeting. Personal likes and dislikes play as great a role here as in other human endeavors, however much the machinery may try to submerge them.[31]

4

European Political Cooperation: Reaching for a Joint Foreign Policy

As if EC matters were not complex enough, the member states have developed a different and remarkable instrument to coordinate their respective foreign policies – European Political Cooperation (EPC).[32] The EPC has become an established part of every member state's foreign policy. It does not – indeed cannot – preclude independent action by one partner, but significant actions taken in isolation, without previous consultations with the other EPC members, have become very rare indeed. A true "consultation reflex" has emerged among the EPC partners, and no one seems willing to jeopardize present commitments to consult before adopting formal positions or launching national initiatives on important international questions of mutual concern.

Beyond the extended commitment to consult, foreign ministers increasingly stress the need to develop a greater potential for joint action. The reason for this is the perceived weakness of the EPC – more reaction than action. And not surprisingly, because it lacks many of the ingredients of a fully fledged foreign policy apparatus, the EPC is not a substitute for foreign policy as it is carried out by its member states. Although it has the long-term potential of becoming that, in the meantime it must still rely on the diplomatic apparatus of its member states. Its real success in establishing itself as a tangible expression of the Twelve's views in the eyes of many foreign countries has led many to expect too much of the EPC. Still an unfinished construction, the EPC is above all an invaluable consultation forum for the Twelve. It has given them the means to act jointly and to publicize their common views whenever they wished to do so. The availability of these means has certainly bolstered the Twelve's will to use them. But consensus still rules, and in many cases divergent opinions have blocked consensus and prevented it from emerging.

Some critics of the EPC have understandably judged it to be an inefficient and purely declaratory instrument. Although partly justified, such criticism completely ignores the reality of the permanent dialogue among the capitals of the Twelve and the evolution in the mentalities and perceptions of the ministers and diplomats involved in its activities. The general foreign policy interests of the Twelve are fairly close. The EPC has reinforced this closeness in many intangible ways; it has given the Twelve a far greater cohesion in their overall approach to international problems. The constant sharing of information and comparison of sources between the member states through the EPC process is an added benefit that has done much to increase the efficiency of their foreign policies. The EPC has thus enabled them to have a greater international impact than would have been the case otherwise. As long as both the limitations and the possibilities of the EPC are understood, the risk of harboring unduly pessimistic or unduly optimistic expectations will remain small.

The EPC is not a part of the institutions set up by the treaties of Paris and Rome. Yet its links with them are numerous and their relations so intertwined that they cannot be considered in isolation from one another. Indeed the EPC is a conduit for the expression of policy attitudes. To back its positions with effective actions, such as aid or trade sanctions, it needs the economic weight provided by the EC. Conversely, the EC's external policies require the overarching political framework provided by the EPC. The main link between them is the Presidency.

A Gradual and Pragmatic Creation

Unlike the EC, the EPC grew in a wholly pragmatic fashion without being established by treaties. It was not legally recognized until the Single European Act was ratified in 1986.[33] Its origins can be traced to the 1969 Hague Summit that finally opened the door to British membership in the EC. The European leaders at that time felt a growing need for the coordination of their external policies, especially in view of the prospective enlargement of the EC from six to nine members. This was seen as contributing to the "ultimate goal of political union."[34] The assembled heads of state and government decided then to entrust their foreign ministers with the task of studying "the best way of achieving progress on the matter of political unification within the context of enlargement. The ministers [were] to make proposals before the end of July 1970."[35]

The foreign ministers finalized their report at their October 1970 meeting in Luxembourg. Because this basic charter of the EPC had been prepared by the political directors in the foreign ministries of the six member states (the Six) under the leadership of their Belgian colleague, Viscount Etienne Davignon, it is known as the Luxembourg or Davignon Report. Its most fundamental option was the choice of foreign policy as the best field for progress toward political unification. To a large extent, this basic premise remains true today. Its objectives were defined as follows:

> • to ensure, through regular exchanges of information and consultations, a better mutual understanding on the great international problems;
> • to strengthen their solidarity by promoting the harmonisation of their views, the coordination of their positions, and, where it appears possible and desirable, common actions.[36]

No obligation other than that of consulting one another was thus entered into by the governments of the Six. The foreign ministers approved the proposed mechanisms, setting up regular meetings of both the foreign ministers and the political directors. The proper subjects for consultation were very broadly defined as follows: "Governments will consult on all important questions of foreign policy. State members may propose any question of their choice for political consultation."[37] Relations with the Commission and the European Parliament were defined in very simple terms, and certain tasks were given to the country holding the Presidency. With these elementary guidelines, the EPC started functioning. Its first ministerial meeting was held in Munich on November 19, 1970. The two first topics on its agenda were the Middle East and the Conference on Security and Cooperation in Europe (CSCE). Both are still there today. The first joint action of the Nine in an international forum took place in January 1973 at the preparatory meeting to the CSCE Helsinki Conference, which in effect marked the appearance of the EPC as an actor on the international scene.

Since its modest and pragmatic beginnings in 1970, the EPC has evolved considerably, mainly through a constant strengthening of the consultation requirement.[38] Several additional reports were adopted by the foreign ministers in Copenhagen in 1973 and in London in 1982. In addition, the 1975 Tindemans Report on European Union and the 1983 Stuttgart Declaration devote significant sections to the EPC before its present codification in the Single European Act. Every one of these documents has meant further substantial progress, which has now reached the point at which joint action by the Twelve has clearly become a desirable goal of the EPC.[39]

The desirability of adopting and implementing common European positions is among the goals defined by the Single European Act. That these common positions serve as *the* framework for their external policies has been apparent for some time now. Many European commentators, mindful of the gradual removal of historical obstacles, consider this evolution to have been a success story. Thanks to the EPC, the Twelve have achieved common positions and a recognized status with regard to most, if not all, of the main international issues.

The Organization of the EPC

To understand the functioning of the EPC and the role played by the Presidency requires a brief review of the way it is organized today. (Also see the appendix to this volume.) The EPC's basic building blocks are the approximately 20 *working groups*. Their members are mostly diplomats – foreign ministry heads of department – dealing with the various groups' areas of responsibility. They meet in Brussels, at the seat of the secretariat.[40] Regional groups deal with Africa, the Middle East, Central and South America, Eastern Europe, and Asia, and thus cover the whole world except for North America.

Thematic groups handle such subjects as the United Nations (UN), the CSCE, disarmament, human rights, and terrorism. Functional groups discuss matters of mutual operational concern, such as the setting up of common radio networks in some of the more remote diplomatic posts abroad, the running of the common telecommunication system linking the Twelve together, and common visa problems. Every group has a mandate from the Political Committee and reports to it.

A noteworthy degree of cooperation has developed over the years between the heads of various departments. They meet regularly, once a month for the most active groups such as the Middle East group, several times during the six-month term of the Presidency for most others, and less often than that – but at least once every six months – for the rest. International developments often dictate more frequent meetings. There is a total of about 100 to 120 working group meetings a year. Useful as they undeniably are, the working groups suffered until recently from their lack of permanent administrative support. There are physical limitations on the ability of department heads to be away from their offices for meetings in Brussels. The establishment of the secretariat, which will be discussed shortly, has helped somewhat. But the need for a more permanent setup will probably make itself more acutely felt at some time in the future.

The *European correspondents* are a special group. As direct assistants of the political directors, they have the special tasks of maintaining a liaison with their counterparts in the other foreign ministries and making sure that the EPC functions smoothly inside their own ministry. Meeting at least once a month, right before the Political Committee, they also are frequently in contact by telephone to iron out the wrinkles in the system. As the coordinators of the EPC inside their foreign ministry, they make sure that answers and instructions are drafted on time, that the political director—and where appropriate the minister—has approved them, that the right people attend the right meetings, and so forth. The Political Committee relies on the correspondents for other special tasks that it assigns from time to time, such as monitoring the development of cooperation among the Twelve's embassies abroad.

One of the most efficient instruments of the EPC, the COREU (Correspondant Européen) telex network, is directly supervised by the correspondents. Permanently linking the capitals of the Twelve and the Commission, this classified network enables the Twelve to consult rapidly with one another in times of crisis. It also serves to prepare common declarations and voting instructions in the UN and elsewhere, to exchange views and information on any topic, and to organize the many EPC meetings. Roughly 6,000 telexes a year transit this network, which is also connected to the Twelve's permanent missions in New York and Geneva. The correspondents must be reachable at all times, because the network is open 24 hours a day.

The linchpin of the EPC is the *Political Committee*, or POCO, as it is known in English. Its members are the political directors of the Twelve, equivalent to the under secretary for political affairs in the U.S. State Department. As is the case in the working groups, a representative of the Commission is always present.[41] The successor of the Davignon Committee, POCO "is the central coordinating body of the EPC. It directs the working groups and prepares the ministers' decisions. It oversees the whole of the Twelve's foreign policy activities; it also exchanges views and prepares common declarations and positions."[42]

The POCO meets at least once a month for its regular meetings, except in August. It also gets together on the eve of the meeting of the UN General Assembly to finalize the speech to be delivered in the name of the Twelve by their presiding foreign minister. And POCO meets during the twice yearly gatherings of the European Council to put the final touches to the draft declarations on international problems that are a normal feature of European Council communiqués. International gatherings attended by the Twelve are also frequently used by POCO as a further opportunity to meet. During an average year, the political directors will have had nearly 20 meetings. Normal monthly meetings usually take a day and a half and are held in the capital of the country holding the Presidency or at the seat of the newly established EPC secretariat in Brussels. Crisis meetings, which have occurred several times already, may be called on 48 hours' notice at the request of three member states.

POCO members know each other very well. They form an intelligent fraternity in which differences and viewpoints are aired, at times with considerable frankness. As is always the case in such a group of talented people, personal rivalries are sometimes felt, but remarkably they have proven to be more of a stimulus than a damper. POCO is an influential body whose recommendations carry considerable weight with the foreign ministers. The better foreign diplomats know this well and make persistent efforts to keep in close touch with its activities. POCO members have to draw a line between what legitimate information can be given to allies and like-minded countries after each meeting and what must be kept confidential until ministers have had a chance to discuss the issue or the recommendation they have received from POCO.

The next rung upward on the EPC pyramid is the *ministerial meetings*, where decisions are usually made or formalized. Except when circumstances or time constraints prevent them from waiting until their next ministerial meeting and force them to reach consensus through the COREU network, ministers will meet to adopt common declarations and common positions on the more important issues. They will issue joint instructions to their missions abroad or to the political directors. They are appraised of progress in the various sectors of EPC activity, which enables them to set the future lines of policy or to reconcile differences that remain at the POCO level.

Ministers also meet frequently to discuss EPC matters. Four yearly meetings are scheduled, two in the capital of the country holding the Presidency and two on the occasion of a regular EC General Affairs Council meeting, either right before it or just after it. But ministers nearly always use the other General Affairs Council meetings to discuss pressing international issues. They meet twice a year in informal weekend sessions known as "Gymnich-type" meetings (the first one was held in the German official guest house in Gymnich). They also meet twice in the framework of the European Council and once on the occasion of the UN General Assembly.[43] In effect they thus meet at least 15 times a year on EPC subjects for an average total of 20 days, to which one must add their EC meetings. The same provisions for the convening of crisis meetings apply to the ministerial meetings as they do for POCO. European foreign ministers also know each other well, with all the advantages and drawbacks of such familiarity.

At the summit of the EPC pyramid is the *European Council*, which is covered more fully in chapter 6. At the root of the EPC because of the 1969 decision, the European Council has also developed because of the success of its offspring. Because the need to coordinate EC and EPC activities soon became apparent and no common institutions were on hand for this purpose, it quite naturally fell to the heads of state and government to take up the task. Regular meetings became necessary, which led to the replacement of the rather informal and loosely structured European Summits by the more formalized and systematic European Council meetings. These meetings of the prime ministers of the Twelve are now called upon to give the necessary impulse to the development of the European Union and to coordinate its activities. The European Council also solemnly states the common standpoints of the Twelve on important international issues. Many of the more significant European positions have been formally adopted at European Council meetings, one of the best known being the 1980 Venice Declaration on the Middle East. In the recent past, though, the prime ministers have dealt more often with internal problems stemming from budgetary constraints and the enlargement of the EC. They have been usually content with the adoption of statements prepared for them by POCO and approved by the foreign ministers. Their informal meetings, however, have frequently been used to broach international issues, with one of their favorite topics the evolution of the Soviet Union and the relationship of the superpowers.

Several other elements of the EPC must also be mentioned to obtain a comprehensive picture:

Relations with the European Parliament have been a feature of the EPC since the start. Twice during every Presidency, the presiding foreign minister holds a meeting with the Political Committee of the European Parliament. He informs it fully on EPC activities and fields the numerous questions its members raise. The minister also has to answer questions in the monthly plenary session of the European Parliament (see chapter 7).

Various formats for contacts with third countries have been developed by the EPC. The Presidency is solely responsible for this, but experience has shown that in some instances one-on-one meetings (the Presidency alone with whatever foreign nation) are not the ideal format. Some special political emphasis might be required, the continuity of the EPC might have to be stressed, or more public exposure might be called for. Deploying all of the Twelve can only be accomplished in very rare instances, agendas being what they are.

The "troika" format thus was born, which regroups the acting President with both the former and succeeding presidents and the Commission. All kinds of variations on this format have taken place.[44] It is a useful tool. Some countries are more comfortable talking to three Europeans, whom they might consider to represent a good cross-section of the Twelve, rather than just one who, however faithfully he might present the Twelve's views, might be perceived as lacking a clear mandate on some issues. Some of the Twelve have also been known to feel better with three partners representing them instead of just one.

The *embassies of the Twelve* also play a part in EPC activities. A distinction must be made between the embassies in another member state of the EC and embassies in third countries. The missions operating in another member state are integrated with the activities of the EPC. They receive copies of all but the most confidential COREU telexes through the local Foreign Ministry and are systematically informed by it of the results of visits made abroad by leading ministers and officials of that country as well as of conclusions drawn from incoming visits.[45] Their reports to their capitals help prepare forthcoming discussions within the EPC. They also serve as a complement to the COREU network, distributing documents too bulky for telex transmission. And in many EC capitals, the foreign minister has regular contact with the ambassadors from the other member states, especially before important EC or EPC meetings.[46]

In third countries, the Twelve have developed systematic cooperation among their embassies.[47] Ambassadors and their aides meet on a regular basis to exchange information, prepare common reports, or carry out joint demarches following instructions received from the Political Committee via the capital of the current president. This is particularly intense in the major international organizations, especially in the UN and its agencies in New York and Geneva, which explains why these missions have a permanent link with the COREU network. In times of heavy activity, such as a General Assembly or a special session, the heads of missions or their main aides meet every day.

Successful cooperation depends to a large extent on the individual diplomats posted abroad. Some of them still have reflexes of an earlier but not so distant era of competition rather than cooperation. To help overcome some of their nationalistic inhibitions, POCO has issued detailed instructions on the areas of cooperation and the actions to be taken.[48]

Until January 1, 1987, the EPC had operated without a headquarters and without permanent staff. The correspondent in each Foreign ministry was the only official permanently on top of EPC business. As the Presidency rotated, so did the weight of running the EPC, which literally went from one capital to the next in a process described as "the flying Presidency." Some measure of continuity was introduced when a diplomat from the previous and the next presidencies were assigned to the Foreign Ministry in the Presidency capital, but that arrangement was too ad hoc to work satisfactorily. The Twelve thus decided to set up a small, permanent EPC secretariat. Based in Brussels, in the EC Council of Ministers' building, it is separate from the Secretariat General of the Council but draws upon it for logistical support.[49] The EPC secretariat is headed by a senior diplomat appointed for two and a half years, at present an Italian appointed in January 1987. He is assisted by five diplomats drawn from the two preceding presidencies, the present one, and the two succeeding ones in rotation. Each of the five thus serves for two and a half years, a replacement coming in every six months.

The existence of the secretariat has measurably helped in shouldering a very heavy burden, especially in preparing and running the meetings, as well as in drawing up the draft answers to parliamentary questions. The Belgian Presidency — first to benefit from it — has certainly found it useful to rely on this newly established secretariat, which has proved its worth in a very short time. A more definitive judgment will have to await the results of the experience of working out of Brussels with several presidencies based in other capitals.

An exclusive instrument of the Presidency, the secretariat has seen its functions defined by the Single European Act. They are "to assist the Presidency to prepare and carry out the activities of the EPC and to discharge its administrative responsibilities, under the authority of the Presidency," thus directly strengthening it.[50]

The EPC is run entirely by diplomats and does not have any legislative effect in the member states, as opposed to the EC, in which experts from many different departments take part in the activities of the working groups of the Council before it enacts legislation applicable in all the member states. That explains why the EPC operates with only two languages, English and French. All meetings, except at the ministerial level — where the Germans speak German and most others speak either of the two EPC languages — are run in these two languages exclusively, and all the COREU traffic carries messages in nothing but English and French.[51] This undoubtedly eases and speeds up the work of the EPC. People who have had the experience of working in both the EC and the EPC invariably comment favorably on this aspect of the EPC.

The Presidency and the EPC

It is interesting to focus now on the role of the Presidency in the EPC and to compare it with its EC functions.[52] Bear in mind that the EPC does not have the elaborate institutions of the EC, even though the members are the same and the Presidency is exercised by the same country. From the start, the EPC Presidency found itself playing roles that were initially those of the EC Commission.

The function of the EC Presidency was never even speci-
fied in the original EC treaties. The growing importance of
the Presidency's role is due to another phenomenon – the
erosion of the Commission's powers over several years. We
have seen how complex the management of the various
councils and the enlarged EC has become. The emergence of
the European Council, under French prodding, reflected the
French taste for strong presidential powers and their dis-
taste for too strong supranational institutions, as epito-
mized by Prime Minister Charles de Gaulle during the 1965
"empty chair" crisis. (Because de Gaulle wished to stop
what he saw as a dangerously irreversible trend toward
more supranationalism, France did not attend Council
meetings between July 1965 and January 1966.)

In addition, the EC gradually outran the treaties. New
fields of competence were added to it that had not been
foreseen by the treaties, thus reducing somewhat the powers of the Commission, especially in the management of the
EC. Several weak Commissions, fearful of unduly antagoniz-
ing the major member states, let some of their most basic
prerogatives fritter away in this context, which is why the
Presidency now assumes tasks that were initially the sole
responsibility of the Commission. Their similarity with the
EPC presidential functions is obvious, but this near identity
reflects different institutional developments.

Indeed, in the case of the EPC, one can argue that the
Commission managed to extend its powers from those of a
merely tolerated observer to the point of having become a
full participant in the discussions and even a privileged one,
because it is the only permanent troika member. It does
not, however, take part in the decisions that, by their nature, are the prerogative of the member states.

As the EPC acquired more and more substance, the functions of its presidents grew correspondingly, turning the
Presidency into the major instrument of political cooperation. Its principal tasks are the following:

1. It serves as the driving force or initiative taker, a role
assigned to the Commission by the EC treaties. The Presi-

dency establishes the agendas of the meetings and prepares the working documents circulated to partners ahead of the meetings. It chairs meetings and introduces the discussions, thus providing initial impetus and direction. It also drafts the conclusions of the various meetings, an important task because future courses of action and instructions to the Twelve's representatives are based on these conclusions. At the end of every meeting, the proposed conclusions are sent to partners. If they do not disagree within 48 hours, the conclusions become definitive. To limit the risk of ma;or differences, the Presidency shows its draft conclusions to the correspondents at the end of each POCO meeting and to the political directors at the end of each ministerial meeting. Their comments and reactions are embodied in the COREU message sent that same evening to all capitals.

2. The Presidency also assumes important administrative functions because it runs all the meetings and determines their frequency. The COREU network is managed by the communications department in the presidential capital. The Presidency is responsible for updating the rules book that goes by the significant name of *Coutumier* (a term similar to "standard operating procedures").[53]

All the costs deriving from the exercise of the Presidency are borne by each country successively. Some presidencies are more expensive than others, depending upon the international situation and the incumbent's talents in persuading his colleagues to let him take new initiatives abroad in the name of the Twelve.

The Presidency must also make certain that there is common agreement on the draft answers to the parliamentary questions and must ensure that its representatives abroad have received the necessary instructions to implement the latest EPC decisions.

3. In contrast to the EC, all EPC decisions reflect consensus. The Presidency must continually wheel and deal to coax reluctant partners and push them towards compromises that a majority see as desirable. In some instances the Presidency will find itself first trying to put a majority

together. This rule of unanimity is a major constraint on more successful EPC activities.[54] It taxes any president's negotiating skills; thus one cannot emphasize too much the importance of his personality and determination. A strong, capable, and tactful president will get the needed support and cooperation from his colleagues.

4. The Presidency is also responsible for the correct and efficient implementation of EPC decisions, an important and nearly exclusive role carried out through its diplomatic apparatus. Demarches, common statements, contacts, diplomatic missions abroad or in its home capital are all tasks that fall upon the Presidency collectively.

5. From the beginning, the Presidency has been entrusted with the role as spokesman of the EPC before the press, Parliament, and third countries as well as international bodies. In the UN General Assembly, the Twelve rotate their allocated speaking slots to allow the president to speak before all his other colleagues and in their common name.

The Presidency is either alone in contacts with third countries, or it heads the troika or, much more rarely, the full comity of the Twelve. It always expresses itself on their behalf. In some cases, it has a fairly comprehensive and detailed position to articulate. In other instances, when a mere outline of the common attitude is available, the president is free to present the Twelve's views as he sees fit. As far as Parliament is concerned, the Presidency also speaks on behalf of the Twelve during the question time or in special debates on the activities of the EPC (see chapter 5).

At the end of every ministerial meeting, the president meets with the press and gives an outline of the most significant decisions and discussions. He usually adheres to agreed-upon press guidelines whereby no common statements or positions have been adopted, either because of a lack of consensus or, more frequently, because of the absence of a need for a formal common stand at that moment on any given issue. He must carefully refrain from giving details considered confidential or from identifying dissenting partners on an unresolved issue. With so many member states, confidentiality is not easy to maintain. Leaks to the media are commonplace from both Brussels and the capitals.

The Presidency of the EPC is thus no small task; it taxes the whole external apparatus of the country in charge. Although easier for the larger member states because of their more numerous personnel, it is a heavy load on the smaller countries. The introduction of a secretariat has helped in this respect. But the existence of the EPC and of the rotating Presidency has forced all of its members, large or small, to think in global terms and thus to open themselves up to all of the international issues, whether or not their national interests are directly involved.

To speak of the Twelve as solely concerned with regional issues is thus wide of the mark. The strengthened commitment to joint action implies a more significant EPC role in the future. And the time will certainly come, as it must if the Twelve want to retain a significant international identity, when the constraining consensus rule will start eroding. Member states might finally agree—as has been recently suggested—to abstain on issues that are not of major concern to them, if they find themselves in the position of blocking the adoption of common positions. The pressure of external events will doubtless step up the pace toward increased European integration. Most great strides in that direction have indeed been achieved under the pressure of external events seen as potentially damaging to the EC—for example, the Korean War, the Hungarian uprising of 1956, the Suez fiasco, and, more recently, the Reykjavik Summit.

5

The EPC and European Security

The ongoing debate about Europe's security has been closely linked to the EPC. It is a common mistake to believe that the EPC has remained aloof from security issues until recently. Quite the contrary is true, even though the EPC's attempts to expand fully into the field of security have been dogged by ambiguity and failure. The limited results that have been achieved and the unpromising prospects for future progress explain the successful revival of the Western European Union (WEU), discussed later in this chapter.

The EPC and the CSCE: A Success Story

The EPC's one undisputed success so far has been its role in the CSCE, a process that has involved all 33 European states and Canada and the United States, the North American states with European interests.[55] Ever since it began, the EPC has coordinated its member states' positions on CSCE topics, which have been divided into three clusters. The second cluster of topics, economic issues, was prepared by the EC in the normal framework of the Council. The EPC coordinated the positions of its member states for the first cluster, which was on security issues, as it did for the third one – the issues concerning the freedom of movement within Europe (most basic human rights fall within this category). The EPC has monitored this process as it evolved after the signing of the Helsinki Final Act in July 1975. Italian Foreign Minister Aldo Moro signed the act in his dual capacity as Italian representative and president of the EC Council of Ministers. Moro stressed that the EC had committed itself to the correct implementation of the act "in the matters for which it is presently competent as well as for the matters to which its competence will extend in the future."[56]

The degree of cohesion maintained by the EPC throughout the different stages of the CSCE process has been most remarkable in the view of strong potential for divisions among the EPC partners. Indeed, some of the issues went right to the heart of Germany's interests; others made life uncomfortable for the French because of their specific approach to European security and East-West relations and for the Irish because of their neutrality. That none of them prevented the EPC from playing an efficient, and at times a leading, role must be counted as a success.

The EPC's leading role was most prominent in the early stages of the conference, when the West was still attempting to define its positions. The EPC countries managed to convince their other Western partners, foremost among them the United States, that this conference dealt with problems that were more directly relevant to Europe and that they therefore had to take the main responsibility for drafting the Western position papers. The cohesiveness of the EPC, both within the Western group and in the conference at large, did much to establish its international credibility. This was not achieved without problems – for example, the constant shifting back and forth between the EPC and NATO caucuses in an attempt to harmonize positions between two groups with different memberships and political emphasis. Unfortunately this very real EPC success in dealing with security matters has been limited to CSCE.

Why then has the EPC managed to accomplish even

this, given the strong potential for discord among its members? Two basic reasons spring to mind – the security issues developed within CSCE as the process evolved and, more fundamental, the importance that all EPC partners attribute to East-West relations. Because of this essential ingredient of any European country's foreign policy, the EPC had to become actively involved in the CSCE, or it would have quickly ceased to be relevant to some of the most basic preoccupations of its members.

The International Scene: Limited Success

The EPC has managed to address security issues in other more limited instances, but never continuously. In most cases, the EPC merely reacted to an international event viewed as potentially damaging to the Twelve or to one of them. To EPC partners, the concept of security encompasses a broader framework than a purely military one. Terrorism became an immediate preoccupation. And other events geographically more removed were also addressed because of their long-term political or economic security implications for the Twelve.

Poland

Following the state of emergency and the establishment of military rule in Poland in December 1981, the Ten, as the member states then were known, decided to impose sanctions on that country. This was only done in January 1982, nearly a month after the events in Poland. The EPC made the political decision, and COREPER put together the package of sanctions, producing in the process a textbook example of the complementarity between the EPC and the EC. But the Ten had reacted slowly. And their cohesiveness was not perfect, because the Greeks decided they wanted no part in any sanctions against Poland. The slowness in the EPC's reaction had one beneficial consequence, however; it led to the decision to establish a mechanism to convene meetings at short notice.

The Falklands

Another instance of EPC involvement in matters of security was the Falklands War of 1982. The UK requested and received, as a gesture of solidarity, the full support of its EPC partners, and sanctions were imposed for a short time on Argentina, again in conjunction with COREPER. But in this instance also, some member states experienced difficulties in going along with the majority. Ireland and Italy, for different reasons, either did not impose sanctions or lifted them before the others did.[57]

Syria and Libya

In two other cases connected with terrorism, both involving the UK, the EPC managed to arrive at common positions. Sanctions were imposed upon Libya in 1984 as a result of the fatal shooting of a policewoman in London by a member of Libya's People's Bureau. When it became clear that official Syrian operatives were involved in the plot to blow up an Israeli airliner about to take off from London's Heathrow airport in 1986, sanctions were also applied to Syria.

Both incidents, together with the bombing of Tripoli by the United States, spurred the Twelve toward a much greater degree of cooperation in the fight against terrorism.[58] But political differences again prevented them from acting in total unison. Until the Libyans fired a missile at the Italian island of Lampedusa, without hitting it, the Italian government had always been fairly reluctant to adopt sanctions that would really hurt Libya. Besides, it was generally recognized that, although certainly a source of terrorist actions, Libya was not, by far, the worst offender. Greece, however, stated that it had always maintained special and privileged relations with Syria, which it was reluctant to jeopardize. Many other EPC partners also believed, at the beginning of 1987, that sanctions had been effective, because the Syrians had taken steps to remove the more dangerous terrorist groups from Damascus. They wanted to reintroduce Syria in the diplomatic game of the Middle East because of their February 23 agreement to promote an international conference on the Middle East.[59] They believed that without Syrian participation the proposed conference did not stand a chance of success. The UK blocked the reestablishment of diplomatic contacts for a longer period than would have been wished by most of its partners.

The Middle East

The Twelve have always followed developments in other regions of the world with an eye toward security implications. They have, for example, followed the multiple aspects of the conflict in the Middle East, whether it was the overall Arab-Israeli confrontation, the war in Lebanon, or the Persian Gulf situation. Some of the member states have had contingents in Lebanon (the British, French, and Italians) in the unsuccessful multinational force deployed together with the U.S. forces. The Dutch, the French, and the Irish continue to take part in the UN Force in Lebanon (UNIFIL). Others participated in the 1984 operation to clear the Suez Canal from mines. Still others take part in the naval operations in the Persian Gulf.[60]

Africa

Since the failure of cooperation between the Belgians and the French in the 1978 Kolwezi operation, the attention given to Africa has been better coordinated. (At the Zairian mining center of Kolwezi, Belgian paratroopers had tried to rescue the white hostages of rebels while French paratroopers had tried to strike at rebels vanishing in the bush.) Information on the security implications of developments in Africa are regularly discussed by the foreign ministers and the political directors. Not surprisingly, South Africa,

Namibia, and Angola are recurring themes. The security implications for the Twelve are indeed important from any point of view. In addition, the EC has a substantial aid program in the framework of the ACP conventions, the bulk of ACP members being African states.

Asia and Latin America

The Twelve have repeatedly called for a Soviet withdrawal from Afghanistan and for a Vietnamese withdrawal from Kampuchea. Regular discussions are held with the ASEAN countries and China on these and other political subjects. The main security emphasis for the Twelve is economic, but the effect of a serious deterioration in the internal situation of the Philippines on the U.S. posture in Asia is also a matter of concern.

Central America

A dialogue between the EPC and the five Central American countries (Costa Rica, El Salvador, Guatamala, Honduras, and Nicaragua), together with the Contadora countries (Mexico, Panama, Venezuela, and Colombia), was initiated in 1983 and has become a permanent feature. The Europeans have been made to feel some resentment from Washington for what has been seen as encroachment and insensitivity concerning a region described as America's backyard. The Europeans reply that they are in effect helping the United States by offering these countries the possibility of establishing a political dialogue with other democracies. They also argue that the lure of EC aid, when withheld from countries in a state of conflict, provides an incentive to stability. European interest in the region does not stem primarily, as some U.S. critics contend, from self-serving economic motives.[61] Although certainly not absent, they take a second seat to the overall concern of the Twelve about the possibility of U.S. military involvement in this region at a time of stretched budgets and growing emphasis on conventional defense in NATO. For that same basic reason, the situation in Mexico and its possible implications on U.S. attitudes and policies has frequently been addressed by the EPC. The recent addition of Spain and Portugal to its ranks will also foster a more permanent interest in Latin America.

Certain other international issues are hardly ever discussed by the EPC because they are considered to be part of the military aspects of security. When they do arise, it is either because the issue was thought to be so pressing that the foreign ministers wanted to take immediate advantage of a long-scheduled EPC meeting to address them or because of the more informal, and thus confidential, character of some of their meetings. Problems related to the intermediate-range nuclear force (INF) properly belong to NATO. One single exception to this rule was the briefing given in July 1980 by the German foreign minister to his colleagues in the EPC on the outcome of the talks German Chancellor Helmut Schmidt had just held with the Soviet leadership in Moscow. This was the first encounter between a Western leader and the Soviets since the NATO decision to deploy the INF missiles, and the issue was considered sufficiently important to all members to be discussed in the EPC. The attitudes of some member states prevented this from recurring, but the Gymnich-type informal meetings have time and again been used to raise such topics. The same is true of the informal encounters between the prime ministers on the occasion of European Council meetings. None of these meetings, however, lead to decisions. They offer their participants an opportunity to exchange views and to expose their particular preoccupations. Artificial constraints on topics make no sense in such an environment.

The EPC and Security: The Second-Best Alternative

The inescapable conclusion from this listing of past EPC activities is that the EPC has, with the exception of CSCE and terrorism, failed in significantly addressing security issues except through discussions that were long on political substance but short on practical security-related decisions. A majority of EPC members has been dissatisfied with this state of affairs, which many commentators attribute to the collapse in 1954 of the European Defense Community and the ensuing reluctance to risk another damaging failure. Partially correct, this explanation cannot suffice today. Thirty-four years and another political generation have passed since then. Conditions have changed radically within the Atlantic Alliance and in the world.

Recognizing these changes, the 1975 Tindemans Report was the first to raise the issue again and to state that "security no longer can be isolated from the European Union."[62] The whole report had been considered to be premature at the time; only in recent years has serious attention been given to most of the report's recommendations. The EPC tried unsuccessfully on various occasions to enlarge its mandate to encompass security, getting only as far as a commitment to discuss the economic and political aspects of security, but not its military aspects.[63] These numerous discussions made it clear that several member states did not want to include security issues in the work of the EPC.

Loath to abandon its neutrality, Ireland feared that to address security problems within the EPC would be tantamount to indirect NATO membership. The absence of a solution to the long-festering crisis in Northern Ireland also played a major role, both issues being related and linked to the establishment of the Republic of Ireland.

Greece has contended that there is no need for European involvement in security affairs. Athens is exclusively preoccupied with Turkey and dissatisfied with NATO because of its lack of support in its dispute with Ankara. It also takes a rather benign view of Soviet intentions and has tried to develop a Balkan policy that would be inconsistent with NATO attitudes. Its representative in one of the many discussions on security and European integration quite flatly stated that Greece's sole interest lies in confronting the Turkish threat. Already a so-called footnote state in NATO jargon because of its continuous dissent with NATO communiqués, Greece has also irked its EPC partners with isolated attitudes on policies concerning the Middle East, the fight against terrorism, and relations with Eastern Europe.

The attitude of Denmark is altogether more complex. Its government is not hostile to security discussions within the EPC, but it has to contend with a majority in its parliament that is opposed to any further progress toward European integration. A majority of Danes were lukewarm about the idea of joining the EC in the first place and only agreed to do so because Denmark's main market, the UK, was joining. In addition, Nordic solidarity has a strong pull, dominated by Swedish and Finnish neutrality and by the absence of Norway from the EC. Because of the foregoing attitudes, the WEU was revived from its moribund condition and expanded to become what it is today.

The Reawakening of the WEU

In 1983, both France and Belgium came to the conclusion that the EPC could not fulfill their aspirations for an effective security dimension to European integration. The long-forgotten WEU, though comatose at that time, was still breathing and had all the necessary infrastructures – a small staff, a functioning assembly, and treaty provisions for a council. The WEU thus offered the forum in which security issues could be discussed among Europeans and be made the object of public debate. One added, major attraction was its limited membership – Belgium, France, Germany, Italy, Luxembourg, the Netherlands, and the UK. To put it bluntly, the WEU coincided with the EPC minus the "difficult" countries; WEU members shared similar defense problems in Europe, because all were active in the Central Front region except Italy. To Brussels and Paris, the WEU was a European instrument that would enable the EC core members to coordinate their security policies without being hamstrung by the EC perimeter. Their vision has paid off.

The revival of the WEU was greatly enhanced by the October 1986 Reykjavik meeting between U.S. President Ronald Reagan and Soviet Secretary General Mikhail Gorbachev. Up to then, doubts had lingered about the WEU, but since then there has been no looking back. Some of the more committed "Europeanists" among its members are careful not to let the WEU develop in such a fashion that any hope of linking it, at some point in the future, with the EC and the EPC would be impossible. That is one of the reasons for the present reluctance to consider the enlargement of its membership. It also explains why Norway did not become a member, because it is not in the EC, and why Spain was left in no doubt before its referendum on continued NATO membership that it could not hope to pull out of NATO and become a member of the WEU.

Spain and Portugal have recently been invited to enter into discussions that could lead to their accession to WEU. Difficult issues will have to be tackled, foremost among them the role played by nuclear forces that has been stressed by the October 1987 declaration of the WEU ministerial meeting.

WEU's revival is thus in part the result of the failure of the EPC to address security problems in all of their dimensions. This failure could herald another development in European integration. As the EC expands, and the EPC with it, the disadvantages of what some consider to be a dilution of the EC's original dynamism could become more and more apparent. The WEU could then take upon itself the role of a political hard core within an expanded and diluted EC—a locomotive pulling the rest of the European train along. This scenario then could very well represent the two-speed Europe about which so much has been written.

Such a development is by no means certain. The prospect of establishing the single unified market by the end of 1992 will, for a time, lay these considerations to rest. But the very attractiveness of the EC, because of its growing success, will make several European states, at present out-side of it, press for membership. The issue of a diluted EC will then revive unless majority voting becomes the general rule in most areas, including the more sensitive and elusive ones, such as monetary integration or tax harmonization.

6

The European Council: The Crowning Touch

At the end of every Presidency, a meeting of the European Council is scheduled, usually in June and December. The European Council brings together the prime ministers and the foreign ministers of the member states as well as the president and senior vice president of the European Commission.[64] Given France's Constitution, the French president always attends, and the second seat alloted to the French delegation at the table is alternatively occupied by the prime minister and the foreign minister.[65]

Usually lasting two days, such a meeting represents a major challenge to the organizational skills of any Presidency.[66] It looms ever larger on the final horizon of the six months' period. It demands growing attention from the prime minister and, as a consequence, from the whole cabinet. European rather than domestic issues tend to dominate the internal debates of countries holding the Presidency or about to do so. A good prime minister will take pains to keep the lid on domestic political squabbles at such times both to keep his hands free for EC business and to save face while he is under European-wide public and official scrutiny. The two 1987 presidencies took steps, for example, to prevent internal political events from interfering with their conduct of the Presidency.[67]

Creating the European Council

Until 1974, the European leaders gathered without fixed timing as the need arose.[68] Their informal meetings were considered a valuable way for the EC leaders to get to know each other better and to air their respective views on European integration without being encumbered by a horde of diplomats and civil servants or overwhelmed by numerous position papers addressing a bloated agenda. These meetings were known as European Summits, a name more evocative of traditional international face-offs than of integration. The need to coordinate newly developing EPC activities with established EC policies gradually became evident, and a decision to replace the rather ad hoc European Summits with the European Council was made on December 10, 1974 at the Paris meeting of the heads of state or government.

French influence for the decision was strong, with French President Valéry Giscard d'Estaing playing an important role in getting the European Council off the ground. The French presidential system that seems to have inspired the new venture has kept cropping up in French or French-inspired proposals as recently as the 1985 Milan European Council.[69] The first European Council met in Dublin in 1975, sporting a cumbersome legal designation: "the Heads of Government Meeting as the Council of the Community and in Political Cooperation." Such an inauspicious name fully met the objective of establishing coordination over the European activities of the Twelve. But it could not and did not stick, and the term "European Council" came into general use.

As established by the Paris decision, the European Council was scheduled to meet three times a year. This decision reflected the usual European compromise. Two gatherings a year were deemed sufficient, but that would have meant that the new coordinating body of European integration would hardly ever meet in Brussels, seat of the EC Commission and, as such, a symbol of integration. To accommodate everybody, it was decided to hold three meetings, one each in the capitals of the two Presidency countries for any given year and one in Brussels.

The European Council's Role

The precise role of the European Council has always been fairly ambiguous. By composition, it is a major political institution, and its history reflects the course of integration in Europe. Because it was supposed to supervise the general direction taken by European integration, the European Council evolved at one point into a sort of European Ministerial Court of Appeals for the difficult issues that normal Council meetings were unable to solve. The more this role was emphasized, of course, the more difficult it became for these councils to make decisions, and a vicious circle was thus created. This led to quite frustrating meetings, with cluttered agendas of questions that could not meaningfully be addressed by prime ministers who had had no direct exposure to the preceding debates and thus no thorough grasp of the issues. Worse, they were left with no time to discuss EC perspectives and general policy.

The first substantial attempt to define the role of the European Council came in 1983 when the prime ministers adopted one of the texts Europeans are so fond of – the *Solemn Declaration on European Union*. This document, laboriously agreed upon and then hedged with restrictions embodied in unilateral declarations, is not one of the more significant in the long series of declarations, statements, and proclamations strewing the path of integration. A good rule of thumb in European matters is that the more solemn the declaration, the more empty it is of true content.

The 1983 Stuttgart Declaration is no exception. Hastily put together, at least in European terms, it came into being with the sole objective of preempting the European Parliament, which was busy at the time hammering out what was to become the draft treaty on European Union. Most governments feared, not without reason, that the European Parliament would adopt a text that would go far beyond what was deemed possible at the time and in so doing would raise both the expectations of the integrationists and the hackles of the anti-integrationists.[70] Europe was then in the throes of a major bout of "Europessimism," induced in a large measure by the endless dispute concerning the UK's contribution to the budget.

The declaration was not successful in this context, to no one's surprise. But some of its elements have turned out to be very useful—for example, the part dealing with the European Council and the definition of its role.

As described by that text, the European Council

- gives a general political impulse to the construction of Europe,
- defines orientations and gives general political guidelines to the EC and the EPC,
- maintains coherence among the various aspects of integration,
- defines new sectors of activity,
- solemnly expresses the common positions on matters of external relations.[71]

Another important decision concerns relations with the European Parliament. Ever since the adoption of the Stuttgart text, the president of the European Council has participated in a debate before Parliament on the outcome of his or her Council (see chapter 7).

The 1985 Single European Act had the same effect on the European Council as it did on the EPC. Formally modifying the texts of the European treaties, it gave legal existence to the European Council, hitherto a political creation. But it did not grant it powers equivalent to those held by the EC councils, and it did not take over the definition of the Solemn Declaration. It merely stated that the "heads of state or of government as well as the president of the Commission" are participants and that they are "assisted by the foreign ministers and a member of the Commission."[72]

The Single European Act also does away with the habit

of holding three meetings a year. By stipulating that it meets "at least twice a year," it fortunately reversed the trend, noted earlier, of turning the European Council into an appellate court.[73] Every Presidency since the conclusion of the Single European Act has, on the whole successfully, managed to avoid embroiling the leaders in technical discussions and rather has them concentrate on major issues in political terms. The recent success of the February 1988 European Council in giving the go-ahead for a new medium-term budgetary system for the EC illustrates the point. The prime ministers have now been able to devote several sessions to the task of establishing the internal market by the end of 1992 and its consequences in many politically sensitive areas. They have not had to arbitrate fairly minor differences referred to them by an EC council.

Preparing for the European Council

It is thus no surprise that the prime minister of the country holding the Presidency devotes a substantial amount of his very precious and limited time to a careful preparation of the European Council. A commanding grasp of the issues as well as of the political power play are essential prerequisites. A touch of diplomacy and attention to the psychological comfort of his formidable guests are additional requirements. Considerable effort goes into such apparently mundane elements as the selection of location, menu, accommodations, and gifts that will be offered to the participants and to the large press contingent that descends upon the city where the meeting is held.[74]

During the session itself, the prime minister receives the assistance of his foreign minister, who has presided over the General Affairs Council's meeting that prepared the European Council and often also over a special session specifically devoted to an in-depth preparatory discussion of some of the more pregnant issues to be addressed by the leaders.

In the period leading up to the European Council, he

will also have been helped by his other cabinet colleagues in the chair of important council meetings, the outcome of which often has a bearing on the European Council and on the balance sheet of the Presidency. Most of these issues will have been raised several months before in cabinet meetings specially devoted to the running of the Presidency.

Last, but certainly not least among his helpers, are the many officials working nearly round the clock on the Presidency team, led by the ambassador presiding over COREPER and by the political director who chairs the Political Committee.

As the date of the European Council nears, the prime minister becomes increasingly involved. Although usually well aware of the main issues that will come up for solutions during his country's turn in the chair, the prime minister's attention to European matters must remain more limited than that of some of his colleagues, especially the foreign, agriculture, and finance ministers. He simply cannot put aside for six months all of the domestic issues that cry out for his consideration, even though more than one prime minister has used the Presidency argument to hold down some of the domestic pressures.

In the weeks preceding the European Council, the prime minister normally does the rounds of the 11 other capitals or, at the very least, has previous personal contact with his colleagues whose countries are likely to prove difficult on a sensitive subject. The media exposure he generates in so doing is a powerful incentive to go ahead with these short trips, unless the domestic situation is too dire for that. He also maintains a very close link with the president of the European Commission.

The best results have been achieved by good teamwork between the Presidency and the Commission. Frequent informal and confidential contacts yield a consensus on how best to steer a difficult issue through the European Council. Such an ideal scenario is not always possible, either because some prime ministers do not see eye to eye with the Commission on many issues or because they prefer to run their own show independently of the Commission. Experience suggests that the latter course of action has not led to memorable successes.

After his round of capitals, a few days before the European Council the prime minister sends his colleagues a letter outlining his views on the topics he wishes them to discuss as well as the manner in which he will address them. This letter in effect constitutes the agenda for the meeting. No formal agenda is sent out in advance because of a desire to preserve the fiction – inherited from the more relaxed days of the informal summits – that the leaders are free to mix their agenda as they see fit. That seems a rather naive notion today, even though a great measure of unpredictability remains inherent in any gathering of prime ministers.

Other Participants

Each country's leading duo is accompanied by an official delegation, limited to 17 members including secretarial support, that is allowed access only to the delegation rooms but not to the meeting room itself. A system of badges of different colors separates the participants in various categories.[75] A complex and tight security system ensures that the rules are observed. There are exceptions, of course. The Presidency is allowed two persons in the room, mainly to ensure correct note taking and to pass information to the liaison agents who are stationed in an adjacent room. In addition, the Presidency receives the help of one Council Secretariat officer for the same purposes, which ensures that a complete and accurate record of the proceedings is available to delegations – a crucial need because much of the succeeding work will be influenced by what was said in the meeting. Painstaking attention is devoted to the conclusions of the Presidency regarding the decisions of the Council. The Commission is also allowed three senior civil servants in the meeting room, an arrangement that epitomizes the interrelatedness of the Presidency and the Commission.[76]

In addition to the official delegation, many countries bring in a large number of people who are part of what is described as the nonofficial or technical delegation and reflect a jockeying for power. Most prime ministers believe they need particular experts because of the Presidency's announced intention of dealing with a given matter; they also want to have a ministerial colleague on hand in addition to the foreign minister, either because of his special knowledge of the issue or, more likely, because they wish to involve that particular colleague in the decision and thus share political responsibility for accepting a less-than-ideal compromise. A variant of that tactic on less-loaded issues is to make room in the delegation for another colleague's trusted adviser, who will be called upon to give an opinion on his boss's thinking and thereby associate him by proxy with the decision.

Support staff is also needed for other special chores. The various spokesmen are an indispensable feature of what is a major media event with all the attendant political fallout. All these factors combine to ensure that large technical delegations are on hand because all these people cannot be accommodated within the limited official delegation. Some member states regularly bring in as many as 200 additional people.[77]

Formal and Informal Meetings

The meetings used to start with a discussion of the economic and social situation of the EC, in effect 12 monologues about the successful policies followed by every prime minister. Recent presidencies have now managed to transform this exercise into a discussion of the actions required of every member state to achieve a greater degree of consensus among their economic policies. The prospects for the internal market have reinforced this tendency toward a more businesslike atmosphere. Other topics are addressed by the leaders according to the Presidency's agenda and to the internal dynamics of the meeting. Forecasts as to the way the meetings are likely to evolve and their outcomes have repeatedly shown themselves to be inaccurate.

As usual, informal meetings play a major role. As they arrive in the country holding the Presidency, the leaders are traditionally invited to an opening luncheon offered by the head of state of the host country. Protocol varies little from one country to the next. The assembling leaders have a first opportunity to exchange private views, which is most useful to the presiding prime minister, who can take precious last-minute informal soundings to check the information gleaned from his preparatory trip to the different capitals. In some cases, he will not have managed to see everyone during that round of trips and now has an opportunity to do so.

Official banquets, however, afford limited opportunities for substantial discussions of great length. Catering to that need, the habit has developed for the prime ministers to hold a "fireside chat" on the first evening of the two-day meetings. Their discussions range freely over one or two topics usually selected by the Presidency, provided the pressure of events does not ensure an automatic selection. The foreign ministers dine elsewhere to discuss the EPC topics that will be presented to the European Council the next day as well as other matters of international relevance. No official is present. Only a few whispering interpreters are on hand. The exchanges can indeed be fairly informal – at least as informal as any meeting of 13 leaders can ever hope to be.

The president of the Commission used such a meeting at the end of 1986 to dramatize the looming financial and structural difficulties of the EC. His pitch certainly struck a chord with the prime ministers. Even though most of them had been fully briefed by their usually competent and well-informed foreign ministers and permanent representatives, some of the basic facts – and especially their political implications – had not really sunk in until they personally heard the president of the Commission confront them with both.

The new direction apparently taken by the Soviet Union is another topic that is frequently discussed in some detail because of its many potentially loaded implications.

At the end of the chat, most leaders are reunited with their foreign minister and senior delegation members to compare notes on both meetings. They have a first look at the EPC draft conclusions for the next morning, think out the next day's likely course of events, and often meet with their national media covering the meeting to convey first impressions and reactions on the day's discussions, including some elements of the chat.

These informal encounters are the only opportunity most prime ministers have of meeting all of their EC colleagues together. They usually are useful, if only for that reason. In-depth conversations have taken place, and a better mutual awareness of each other's constraints, political and otherwise, normally flows from these meetings. But prime ministers are leaders, and personality clashes do occur, especially if one of them thinks the meeting did not take his problems sufficiently into account.

The Outcome

The end of the meeting is marked by a press conference given jointly by the presiding prime minister and the president of the Commission. The conclusions of the Presidency are presented to the press, which usually has received some of the texts well in advance, thanks to numerous leaks, some of which are orchestrated. The leaks even extend to documents that were supposed to remain undisclosed because they had never achieved the necessary consensus. The European Council adheres to the idea that it does not make decisions but only provides for orientations; thereby it labels its decisions "Presidency conclusions," which allows for greater flexibility. Some of these conclusions will have been unanimously agreed upon, erasing any distinction between a conclusion and a decision. In other cases, the General Affairs Council is entrusted with the practical fleshing out of conclusions that were uncertain or were not quite ripe.

In addition, the European Council may give solemn public expression to the Twelve's policies and views on major international questions if the need arises — for example, the Venice Declaration on the Middle East, which was adopted by a European Council. The European Council also may remain silent on international issues, even though the Presidency and several, if not all, member states have been approached by foreign parties eager to enlist a formal declaration of support from the Twelve. There are two main reasons for this silence. First, the Twelve might disagree on the need for a declaration on a given issue, either because their foreign ministers have recently expressed the position of the member states and do not want to debase it by frequent repetition or because they disagree on some related fundamental aspect of policy. A good example of the latter was the heated discussion about the question of imposing sanctions on South Africa.[78] Second, the Twelve might be unable to reach meaningful decisions on some of the more basic internal issues facing the European Council. Many feel that weighty European pronouncements on important international problems will be greeted with some cynicism at a time when the EC has just failed to put its own house in order. This is a classic example of the influence of internal issues on the EC's international relevance and credibility.

The outcome of the European Council meeting is the standard measure of the success of any Presidency. Success generates a favorable image for the outgoing Presidency, but a lack of success mars any Presidency's record, even if the causes of the failure are beyond its control.

One of the last acts of the Presidency is to present to the European Parliament the results of the European Council.[79] This task is entrusted to the prime minister himself, who travels to Strasbourg for that specific purpose.

Frustrated officials, waiting in the corridors of the European Council meetings for the leaders to emerge and fearing all the time that they might commit some irreparable mistake owing to the absence of their qualified advisers, often question the usefulness of the European Council. It is fashionable to deride it and to dismiss it as largely irrelevant — an expensive media event that could more efficiently be replaced by the normal work of the EC councils and the EPC ministerial meetings. Most of these comments are provoked by frustration and bureaucratic reactions to a prime minister's political approach to the issues.

As always, there is some truth to these criticisms. European Councils are frequently considered inefficient by those who expect too much out of them. But because the prime ministers of all the member states regularly gather and compare notes, not only on the progress of European integration but also on their respective economic and social policies, they play an important role in gradually shaping commonly held perceptions and creating a greater convergence of their policies. And they fulfill the reason for setting up the European Council in the first place — the need to coordinate the activities of an increasing number of EC councils with those of the EPC. The European Council is here to stay until it is replaced by something more integrative or it is reduced to irrelevance by the failure of European integration — which does not seem likely at this moment.

7

The Presidency and the European Parliament: An Evolving Relationship

The founders of European integration pursued political objectives even though they started with limited economic goals. The original treaties provided for a parliamentary assembly, with members at first drawn from the parliaments of the member states but directly elected since 1979. Direct elections certainly enhanced the legitimacy of the members, the MEPs, but it did nothing to expand the limited powers of the European Parliament. The Single European Act has been instrumental in bringing about a gradual change, as will become apparent later in this chapter, but the overall feeling of most MEPs is one of frustration caused by the mismatch between enhanced legitimacy and the persistence of limited powers.

The overall image of the European Parliament is one of relative weakness. Most MEPs are unhappy both with their roles as members of Parliament and with the image they project to their electorates. They concentrate their fire on the Council of Ministers, which they perceive as the incarnation of outdated nationalistic attitudes and a brake on faster integration. A recent opinion poll taken in all the member states shows a strong desire for "more Europe."[80] Many earlier polls also revealed widespread discontent with EC institutions and thus with the Parliament as well.

Any Presidency thus has to deal with a Parliament that will give it, at best, the benefit of the doubt. There is no traditional interplay between the European Parliament and an executive counterpart, because governments are not responsible to it and the Commission is appointed by the member states. Even though Parliament has the power to oust the Commission, it has yet to do so; the Commission is its ally in the struggle against nationalism, and ousted commissioners can always be reappointed by the governments. And there are no permanent majorities or minorities in the European Parliament. Votes go one way or the other according to the issues and to the number of MEPs present at a given time.[81]

In the following discussion on the role of the Presidency in its contacts with the European Parliament, one must not forget that the Commission is also an active and permanent actor in the Parliament's proceedings. The Commission is always represented at a high level in the introductory and concluding debates – often by its president or by a senior vice president – and it often plays the lead role in the special debates. And there are question times specifically addressed to the Commission, on different days from the Council's. In the plenary sessions, the Commission is seated to the right of the president of the Parliament while the president of the Council sits on his left, a reflection of the attitude of the Parliament toward these two institutions.

The Debates

The incoming Presidency is supposed to present its program to the Parliament at the outset of its six month's period in office. This task falls to the foreign minister in his capacity as president of the General Affairs Council. Both he and his team will have devoted considerable time, in the five or six months preceding their country's turn in the chair, preparing this program by defining priorities, a process that involves intensive and continuous consultations with many principals. They must certainly consult with the Commission, because it calls the shots as far as new legislative initiatives are concerned, and no Presidency can function without precise knowledge of the proposals the Commission will be presenting. Contacts with the Commission will also help to identify the areas for which Commission proposals are already available and where significant progress is either indispensable, given existing constraints (usually budgetary), or deemed to be within early reach. During this consultation process, the future Presidency will be able to play a role in defining where it most wants to achieve results.

Others in this process are those ministerial departments of the government that take the chair, whose ideas and priorities may not always be in line with the general policy of the incoming Presidency or, if they are, cannot all be implemented because of such other constraints as the overall workload and the limited availability of meeting rooms in the building of the Council.[82] Lively debates often result, first at the bureaucratic level and then in the relevant ministerial committees or even in full cabinet meetings. As was pointed out in the discussion of the roles of the various councils, some ministers are not glad to see their foreign affairs colleague play a leading role. The same phenomenon is at play in the preparation of the Presidency program that will be presented to the European Parliament, in effect the blueprint for the Presidency.

The speech by the foreign minister is usually made during the first session of the Parliament that follows the start of the new presidency, ordinarily in the third week of January or of July. Speeches vary according to the personality of the minister as well as to the outlook of his country on European integration and national parliamentary traditions. Although a speech made by a British foreign secretary will not be similar to one delivered by his Italian colleague, some common habits have evolved. Given the extent of matters relevant to European integration and the wish of all ministers not to leave any one of these unaddressed because of the many special interests represented both in the Parliament and in the various national ministries, the Presidency speech had become in recent times a tedious recital of all the domains, however obscure, in which action was contemplated. To make matters worse, the time available to the minister is limited, if not by express rules then by the attention span of his audience and its desire to get on with the rest of the agenda. Recent presidencies have thus started making more political speeches, focusing on the main issues and emphasizing their dominant preoccupations. Complementing the speech, a comprehensive document is circulated to the MEPs at the start of the session. It details all the fields of action for the next six months as well as the intentions of the incoming presidency for every one of them.[83]

A debate follows the minister's speech during which the various political groups represented in Parliament make comments (nearly always unfavorable), express skepticism as to the feasibility of the program, deplore the absence of provisions for action on some favorite subject, or criticize some of the announced priorities. The time for this is limited, according to the number of seats the groups hold.

The foreign minister then gets a chance to answer. An added touch that makes his life more interesting is the habit developed by the political groups of using for this debate MEPs who are of the same nationality as the minister. Often their party is in opposition at home, and they have no reason to hold their fire. Even if they are not, they must show that their hearts now beat European and find some basis for criticism of the Presidency's presumed parochialism. Unfortunately, some of the MEPs' comments and queries are colored by national, even local, issues. Most ministers — national politicians themselves — take this in stride and concentrate their answers on the truly European issues raised during the debate. As is the case with most beginnings, however, a certain amount of euphoria creeps into the presentation of a new Presidency, though some of the ministers with greater European experience have tried to downplay this.[84]

At the end of the Presidency, two debates are held. In the first, the foreign minister gives an accounting of what has been achieved balanced against the program he presented six months earlier. Criticism from the MEPs is then much sharper, and the euphoria in the opening debate is noticeably absent from the concluding one. Six months is too short a period for any Presidency to make significant progress on a broad front. Success occurs here and there certainly — and some of this can be traced to the exertions of the Commission and of previous presidencies — but accompanied by a fair share of incomplete work, unfulfilled expectations, and outright failures. Attendance at this debate is normally low. Most MEPs are not really interested in hearing what the minister has to say because they know a great deal of it anyway; failures were well publicized in the press when they occurred. And ministers understandably try to make political capital out of their Presidency's successes, not the stuff from which attention-riveting political debates are made. With the rare exception, the debate is a desultory one.

The timing of the concluding debate also tends to limit its interest. Most presidencies attempt to organize "their" European Council at the beginning of their last month in office (June or December) to allow the foreign minister to make a fairly complete presentation of his Presidency's accomplishments. Much of the judgment passed on the Presidency normally hinges on the outcome of the European Council. Owing to problems with the prime ministers' agendas, this is not always possible. The foreign minister sometimes has to make his final speech in Strasbourg before the results of the European Council are known, and thus interest in the debate suffers accordingly.

In the second debate, the prime minister in person gives an assessment of the results achieved at the European Council. The personality of the prime minister and the outcome of the European Council drastically affects the attendance at the debate. Some prime ministers have spoken before a mere 10 percent of the MEPs. Nonetheless, prime ministers dutifully come to Strasbourg for this debate, a sign of the growing political importance attached to the European Parliament or at least to the image of European integration at home. No European prime minister can allow himself to be perceived as ignorant of, or indifferent to, European matters, whether he fosters integration or opposes it.

Question Times

During the rest of the Presidency, the foreign minister will take part every month in one-and-a-half-hour sessions of questions and answers on every conceivable EC or EPC subject. The Presidency acts this time as a spokesman for the Council as a whole in EC matters and for the Twelve member states in EPC affairs. The timing, which is strictly followed, consists of one hour for EC questions and half an hour for EPC questions.

This procedure creates frustration for all concerned. The MEPs have had to put their questions in writing well in advance of the debate. A working group of COREPER has prepared the answers to the questions dealing with the EC. The secretariat of the EPC has circulated draft answers of the COREU network on behalf of the Presidency for the questions dealing with the EPC. Every single formal answer has thus received the prior approval of the member states. The minister then reads a prepared text.

Further questions relating to the same subject are then put to him orally. To answer them, he draws on additional material prepared by officials from the Council Secretariat or from the EPC secretariat. These documents faithfully reflect the views of the Twelve or restate known facts, albeit in some greater detail than in the first answer. Since the acting president of the Parliament can allow as many collateral questions as he or she wishes to, the minister often finds himself pressed, sometimes hard. The documentation in his files and his aides can only provide him with so much additional material to draw upon.[85] He may be totally unfamiliar with many of the very specific issues raised, especially in EC matters where he may face questions on topics dealt with by another council, such as environment or transport. He then is grilled, often in a language other than his own, for an hour and a half.[86]

When hard-pressed, the minister might then give his own view, but he must always make it clear then that he is speaking for himself or for the Presidency, not for the Council as a whole or for the 12 member states. MEPs know this, as do the minister and the press. The whole exercise thus suffers from tedium and poor attendance.

Many presidencies, because of the limited intrinsic interest of this aspect of their contacts with the European Parliament, limit the exposure of their foreign minister to the introductory and the final debates. They entrust the task of answering the question times during the rest of their Presidency to a junior minister. Although some of them have been excellent, MEPs do not like this practice, and such negative reaction has led a few presidencies to make a special point of ensuring the presence of their foreign minister at every monthly question time.

More Contacts, Less Frustration

Fortunately, contacts with the Parliament are not limited to this exercise in frustration. Special debates are held on specific topics, and ministers from the Presidency participate according to the council they chair and the relevance of its activities to the debate. Ministers also put in frequent appearances before the parliamentary commission, who will want to know more about the Council activities in the numerous forums previously outlined. These exchanges are much more informative and businesslike than the formal debates. The foreign minister also has a special meeting with the Political Commission of the Parliament after every EPC ministerial meeting – that is, twice during his term in office. The gamut of the Twelve's external relations are reviewed and debated during these half-day sessions, reflecting the constant interest expressed by the European Parliament in the EPC.

Some of this interest derives from the relative weakness of the Parliament on substantive EC matters and the greater ease with which resolutions can be adopted on foreign matters with some emotional appeal to public opinion. In all fairness, though, much of the interest is genuine and reflects the aspirations of most MEPs for a more active European presence on the world scene. Every Presidency makes a great effort to provide the Parliament with as much information as it can give on the activities of the EPC. But the nature of the EPC lends itself less to parliamentary debates than the more specific and more easily identifiable EC activities.[87] The debates tend on the whole to limit themselves to exchanges of views between the minister and the MEPs on the state of the world and Europe's role in it, with a few critical remarks on the way some of the issues have been handled by the EPC.

Another interesting and satisfying contact is the monthly lunch the foreign minister has with the presidents of the Commission and of the European Parliament, at the latter president's invitation. This is the only regular meeting between the presidents of the three main institutions of the EC. Accompanied by only one aide each, the three principals can then plot the course for the next month's activities, compare notes on sticky issues, and share impressions on the political fortunes of some of their colleagues (an important electoral race is nearly always on in one of the 12 member states). These working lunches are useful, especially when all three participants are determined to have a good working and personal relationship. Many mistakes, actual or impending, are quietly corrected or anticipated, and helpful suggestions are aired.

A good example of such cooperation is the address by

the current president of the European Parliament – the Englishman Lord Plumb – to the assembled heads of state and government at the June 1987 Brussels European Council.[88] Such an opportunity had never been taken before, and fears of a precedent were expressed in some quarters. But the president of the Parliament was able to present the opinion of the Strasbourg Assembly on the issues that the prime ministers were going to tackle – that is, measures needed to ensure the success of both the recent enlargement of the EC and the planned single internal market for the end of 1992. Lord Plumb had used one of the monthly presidents' lunches to sound out his two colleagues on their reactions to this new idea of a presentation to the European Council by the president of the European Parliament.

Flexing Parliament's Muscles

The Single European Act has provided for some narrow measure of codecision, but the Parliament is far from satisfied because only negative powers derive from it.[89] The Parliament will henceforth be able to reject or modify a proposed Council decision in the sectors identified by the Single European Act. In case of rejection, the Council will still be able to adopt it, but only by unanimous vote. In case of modifications requested by the Parliament, the Commission must give its opinion on the proposed modifications, and the Council can then either adopt them with a qualified majority or reject them unanimously. One indisputable effect of these new provisions will be to make the Council more attentive to the opinions expressed by the MEPs; the Presidency will have to organize itself accordingly in the sectors identified by the Single European Act. As a consequence, the Parliament is also beginning to concentrate more on technical and specific issues and less on catchall and slightly irrelevant statements. As its work grows more serious, new procedures have been devised to meet the tight deadlines set by the Single European Act. The new procedure will in all probability encourage a constructive dialogue between the Parliament and the Council, with both presidencies playing an active role in identifying the issues and managing the agendas.

Another provision of the Single European Act provides for the previous consent of the Parliament to all the agreements with third countries, all the association agreements, and any new enlargement of the EC. The Parliament recently demonstrated its determination to use its new powers when it refused, in March 1988, to consent to a renewal of the financial provisions of the existing EC-Israeli agreement. A majority of MEPs wanted to send a clear signal of disapproval to Israel for its policies in the occupied territories and decided that this was the best way to do it.

The Presidency's task of explaining Parliament's decision to any foreign country faced with such an action is something fairly new for Europeans; Americans of course are familiar with this aspect of international relations, given the role of Congress. Any candidate for EC membership also knows that it will have to obtain the agreement not only of all the member states but also of a majority in the European Parliament to attain membership. When Ankara presented its candidacy, the Presidency explained this to the Turks and made sure that the implications were fully grasped.

Recent developments in the institutional relationship between the Parliament and the Council probably will alleviate some of the frustration felt both by the Presidency and the MEPs. But in the long run, the basic relationship between these two EC institutions will have to undergo a fundamental change before some of the deeper frustrations disappear. Such change will require a further strengthening of the Parliament's powers and some evolution in the role and the nature of the Council.

8

The Presidential Team

This chapter focuses upon different, but related, is-sues—the special role of the foreign minister and his team in the running of the Presidency as well as two different concepts of the Presidency.

The Foreign Minister

Although other ministers—the prime minister included—play important roles during the six months of any Presiden-cy, the foreign minister has the major one. In most EC coun-tries, to one extent or another, he and his team form the hub, linking together the spokes of the presidential wheel and making sure it turns despite any obstacles.

The foreign minister is the first to call the attention of his cabinet colleagues to the impending Presidency and its attendant obligations. About a year before his country as-sumes the chair, and even earlier in the more thorough coun-tries, he and his staff submit the first outline as to what the hallmarks of that Presidency should be. The foreign minis-ter's participation in the General Affairs Council will have given him a good overall sense of what to expect in the year ahead because most of the issues are fairly permanent ones.

Although crises may erupt at unforeseen moments, in most instances the elements of such crises have existed for some time, and foreign ministers will have had a chance to discuss them. Ninety to 95 percent of the Council's business is thus quite predictable, though not necessarily easy to accomplish. Differences may also emerge within the government on the future Presidency's priorities. Coalition governments are usually more fickle on that score than single party ones, although differences of opinion between powerful ministers and their respective administrations are a feature of any government.

Apart from the issues, the foreign minister also has to give some attention to the procedures. He has to ensure that all of his colleagues have refreshed their memories on the way things ought to be run, on the interplay between the Commission and the Parliament, and on the necessary discipline to ensure the coherence of the whole. The intervals between the exercise of presidential responsibilities by any one country have grown longer because of increased EC membership. With 12 member states, it now takes six years between turns at bat. By then, most ministers have withdrawn from politics or have new portfolios. This drawback is somewhat softened by their regular participation in the EC councils.

Most new presidents will have had some experience of the issues, the procedures, and the personalities. But running a Presidency is a different matter and will typically be a new and challenging adventure for them. Civil servants and diplomats also are likely to have changed jobs since their country last held the Presidency, even though continuity is the rule in most European bureaucracies that do not undergo the traumatic changes characteristic of incoming U.S. administrations.

A new Commission will also have come into office, and ministers will have to be reminded of the need to consult closely with it, although this is probably less necessary for the councils that meet frequently because of the personal relationships that have been established. New procedures for dealing with the Parliament will also have been adopted, and the MEPs' perceptions of their relations with the Council will have been influenced by many new factors since each new Presidency last held that position – not least by a renewed membership of the Parliament itself, with elections held every five years.

Ministers without the experience of previous presidencies might be tempted to take initiatives on their own without consulting the Presidency's coordination mechanisms. Decisions made by the Agriculture Council, for example, are likely to affect both the financial health of the Community and its external relations and thus require coordination. Coordination is also expected of the Presidency because it is one of the Presidency's most basic assignments, if not *the* most basic. In most countries, coordinating the Presidency at the official level is either entrusted to the foreign ministry or to a special body in which the foreign ministry officials play a leading role. At the ministerial level, personalities play a greater role, but the foreign minister is usually the main actor if only by dint of his membership in the General Affairs Council.

Well before the start of the Presidency, the foreign minister will thus have made sure that the cabinet has discussed the issue and that public opinion is aware of the impending Presidency. Before any of his colleagues, he will have established several personal contacts with the president and the leading members of the Commission. From them he will have been seeking both their personal sense of the global issues likely to surface during his six months in office and their views on the specific issues that more directly concern them. Some might ask why the foreign minister will have had talks with the commissioner responsible for financial matters or with his colleague in charge of regional development. The explanation for this again lies with the role of the General Affairs Council. So many of these issues are interrelated that they must be brought together regularly and looked at in a global perspective. Only the General Affairs Council can do this, with the help of

COREPER. The foreign minister thus has a finger in every important EC pie to an extent that varies from country to country according to each's internal organization.[90]

The foreign minister will also have had contacts with the president of the European Parliament and often with various parliamentary groups, as well as with the MEPs elected in his country. Reviewing procedures has been especially necessary since the Single European Act's new provisions on "codecision" were introduced. Without a good understanding of the procedures and of the underlying and shifting political realities, any Presidency will run into trouble when addressing a Parliament that is basically suspicious of the extent of that Presidency's will to get things done. Efficient coordination is also required from the Presidency because most council presidents are called upon to take part in debates organized by the Parliament. Differences in approaches between members of the same government speaking on behalf of the same Presidency are seized upon by the MEPs and exploited to the full if political mileage is to be made. Preliminary contacts with the different parliamentary groups are becoming a tradition, and foreign ministers are expected to submit to questions from their members on the general approach to be adopted by the future Presidency as well as on more specific issues. Some ministerial colleagues are also invited to present their ideas concerning their areas of competence.

In some member states, a meeting with all the national MEPs is called on the eve of the state's assuming the Presidency. The purpose is to create good will by giving information on the future Presidency's priorities. The MEPs thus have an opportunity to express their own views and reactions on what they perceive to be the main issues of interest to the Parliament. The incoming Presidency can benefit from useful feedback on the mood of the Parliament and avoid some mistakes by doing this, in addition to the good will supposedly generated. During this meeting, both EC and EPC matters are raised.

Because any future Presidency of the EPC is usually

anxious to leave its mark, it plans increased diplomatic activity. The foreign minister will have prepared the ground with some of his colleagues, both within the EPC and in the region of the world where action is envisioned, as well as with interested third parties.

As the main coordinator for the Presidency, the foreign minister also undertakes to visit most, if not all, of his colleagues in the last days of the former Presidency and in the first weeks of his. The idea is to present them with a comprehensive view of the new Presidency's intentions, to sound them out on their concerns, and to try to enlist their support for the new agenda.[91]

In addition to these preparatory activities, media pressure picks up as the Presidency nears. Interviews with the national media and op-ed pieces in the newspapers proliferate. Many other interest groups make themselves heard as media attention awakens them to the imminent change. Well-established groups, who do not need to be reminded because their links with Brussels keep them informed, also target the future Presidency with memos and requests for appointments.[92] A great deal of this pressure is directed at the foreign minister, but special interest groups also target the minister presiding over the council in their area of concern.

Once the Presidency has started, the foreign minister and his team are involved nearly around the clock. A major problem lies in the much intensified need to reconcile classical and conflicting demands. Running the Presidency essentially requires a great deal of time for smooth politicking—that is, spending much time in Brussels or in the office on the telephone, reading special papers, taking part in briefings for the Presidency only, and receiving visitors from the EC and from abroad. But it also demands a lot of traveling, to all the member states at least once (more often than that when difficulty arises) and to the various regions of the world on behalf of the Twelve.[93] Meanwhile, internal politics do not stop, and the purely bilateral problems continue.

The task is daunting for any foreign minister but especially so for one from a smaller member state whose ministry and foreign service lack the depth and resources available to the larger states.

Presidency or Chairmanship?

Exercising the Presidency is no trifling matter. With the responsibility comes considerable exposure. Expectations run high. The media, and certainly the domestic press, follow the EC and EPC activities more or less closely. Ministers, not only the foreign ministers, meet with their counterparts. They are interviewed by radio and TV networks. In short, it is an excellent way of raising one's profile, but it can also lead to acute embarrassment.

Activist governments can be ensnared by the temptation to boast of their plans. Documents and policy papers are leaked; public statements are put out, at times with considerable fanfare. Often, plans are presented before adequate consultation – sometimes before any consultation – with the Commission. This preliminary posturing invariably results in embarrassment.

Other ministers – cabinet colleagues sometimes, but usually ministers from other member states – look with disfavor upon incoming presidents who promise dramatic future achievements, especially ministers who have recently held the Presidency and who, either through no fault of their own or because of their ineptitude, have failed to solve a particular problem. In most instances, that problem simply was not yet ripe for a solution.

Much more fundamental – and hard for activists to accept – is the recognition that any Presidency, however worthy and able, can only influence, at best, 5 to 10 percent of the issues. The rest will resist forward movement, hamstrung by the short duration of the Presidency and built-in inertia.[94] EC legislation has to be introduced by the Commission and not by the member states. It must then be considered by various working groups, both in the capitals and in Brussels, and commented upon by the European Parliament and the Economic and Social Committee. All of this consumes a great amount of time and energy. Keep in mind that, with few exceptions, COREPER has to discuss all these projects before submitting them to the ministers in the various councils.[95] There is just so much an individual permanent representative can absorb in the long hours that are the norm for COREPER.[96]

Some of the wiser governments, mindful of the realities of EC life, adopt a lower profile and consider themselves more the chairman of council meetings than a true president. They take over where the preceding chairman left off, attempt to get as much as possible done on the work at hand, and pass the unfinished business to the next chairman. This does not mean that such governments will not have set their national and EC priorities, usually in close consultation with the Commission. Having identified the areas where progress is possible, they focus on those areas with a better chance of success and certainly less exposure to embarrassment than some of the more publicity-minded presidencies. The same observation holds true for EPC activities. The machinery is of course much lighter here, and events move more rapidly than in EC matters. But the other member states will be quick to detect arrogance in the new Presidency's expectations of its performance, and unpleasant surprises may befall the overconfident.

Although attempts made by incoming presidencies to make a spectacular impact on international problems have not usually met with great success, a solid strategy to that end can pay off. The minister and his political director who believe that something worthwhile can be achieved during their six months in the chair will have carefully surveyed all the elements of the problem, tried to nudge their colleagues and the preceding Presidency in the direction deemed most likely to be the right one, and made intensive diplomatic preparations with the foreign partners most directly concerned. To illustrate this, two recent examples come to mind.

In February 1987, the Twelve made public their support for an international conference in the Middle East and declared their availability to play a role in the various phases of the conference. This was no mean feat, considering the wide range of nuances in the attitudes of the Twelve toward the problem of the Middle East. Agreement was reached in the end, because the timing was judged to be right and all the elements for success were there. But it would not have occurred without intensive groundwork over a number of months before the February 23, 1987 ministerial meeting—help that involved preceding presidencies as well as other partners and foreign governments.[97]

The other example is one of a failure. On South Africa, the Twelve have adopted a fairly standard attitude: declared opposition to apartheid backed up by support for the relevant UN resolutions, as well as by an arms embargo, economic and trade sanctions, travel and visa restrictions, and, more originally, positive support measures for the moderate—that is, nonviolent—black opposition. As always, degrees of enforcement and compliance with sanctions vary. But the Twelve believed that this was not enough. It was all very well for them to tell the South Africans that they were opposed to apartheid, but they had not suggested anything constructive. The Twelve identified the elements that they thought were essential for genuine national dialogue.

The Twelve believed the aim of this dialogue should be the emergence of a free, democratic, nonracial, and united South Africa, which would take into account the diversity of its society and meet the legitimate political aspirations of the majority. While emphasizing that defining the exact shape of new constitutional arrangements was up to the South Africans, the Twelve agreed among themselves that six closely interrelated and mutually supportive basic principles had general validity. Informal contacts showed that other major allies, chief among them the United States,

were interested and thought the document useful and timely. But, one major member state remained adamantly opposed to publishing these principles, thus robbing the
Twelve of any possibility to intervene constructively. All of
the president's strenuous efforts to change this proved to be
in vain; the matter was one of internal political ideology
coupled with a hard-nosed, long-term view of the dissenting
country's interests.

Most presidencies fall somewhere between assertive
and modest. Indeed, most are simultaneously a mixture of
both, depending upon the individual ministers chairing the
various councils. But the overall tone is set out by the foreign minister in his speech to the Parliament at the outset
of the Presidency. An example of a recent attempt to re-
verse the trend toward an increased presidential role is the
speech made before the European Parliament on January
22, 1987 by Belgian Foreign Minister Tindemans. Anxious
to downplay what he perceived as exaggerated expectations of the Presidency's role, he stated: "The member state
which takes on the Presidency cannot by itself impose
progress or inspire an orientation. The authors of the Treaty of Rome, in their wisdom, have reserved this role to the
Commission."[98]

La présidence est morte, vive la présidence

And at the end of six months, overworked ministers and
officials will hand over their tasks to the next country in the
alphabet.[99] Inside the permanent working groups and committees, the transition is easy and smooth. The work proceeds
on whatever was at hand. The foreign minister and his team
meet with the incoming Presidency to compare notes, to allow
it to take advantage of the lessons learned and mistakes avoided, to give information on contacts with some
key players, to review the unfinished business, to give some
discreet advice if it is requested, and so forth. These contacts are valuable. Most of the time both teams know

one another through the council meetings and the use of the troika. As the time to change presidencies draws near, the permanent representatives of both countries will have increased the level of their normally close cooperation and the political directors will have done the same. The incoming Presidency is understandably anxious to benefit from its predecessor's experience. It also can seek to shape the future by requesting help in preparing the ground for some of the incoming Presidency's pet projects.

The outgoing team normally experiences mixed feelings. Relief over shedding the work load is often combined with a tinge of regret at no longer having a hand on the controls of the EC, no longer being so immediately and thoroughly informed by both the Commission and the Council Secretariat, no longer enjoying the exclusive privilege of the excellent presidential briefing papers – in short no longer being in charge and in the limelight.

Whatever the case may be, the Presidency is an experience that leaves no one indifferent. Professional and personal fulfillment are the usual rewards, be it through the rare and prized success or through mere survival over the more frequent frustrations. The ultimate prize to some may be a greater wisdom in the ways of men and in the tortuous paths of European integration. To others it may be a place in history as an architect of enduring change on the road to a united Europe.

9

The Presidency: A Partner in U.S. Relations

In its continuous evolution toward the ultimate goal of a united Europe, European integration has always been supported by the United States. Jean Monnet had many friends in the United States, and most thoughtful U.S. policymakers have held – and still hold – the belief that European integration definitely is in their interest, for a number of reasons. Commonly held values, for example, should be preserved and expanded, such as individual freedom, the rights of man, and true democracy. Strategically, a strong Western Europe can better resist Soviet pressures and exert an influence on Eastern Europe. And economically, an integrated market can offer better possibilities to U.S. exporters than can 12 separate ones with their different legislations. In addition, a cohesive and significant economic entity can help in managing the global economy.

There is, of course, a flip side. As European unity becomes more of a reality, the issues of security and defense will arise, requiring not only a greater shouldering of the common burden by the Europeans but also a greater European role in running NATO. Present international trends tend to reinforce this view, and sooner or later Americans will have to decide whether or not they are ready to contemplate an increased European role within the Atlantic Alliance.

The establishment of a truly integrated European market by the end of 1992 also raises some fundamental questions for the United States. In theory, and probably also in practice, such a move will largely benefit U.S. businesses, exporters as well as European-based multinationals. In regard to the dismantling of EC internal barriers, U.S. trade officials have often expressed fear of a growth of European protectionism that would lead to the establishment of competing mercantilist blocs, with disastrous consequences to the world economy. Although this scenario cannot be entirely discarded, it is unlikely because of the great stake Europe itself has in preserving an open world trading system. The EC is, after all, the world's major trading bloc. A majority of its member states have a vested interest in an open system, even if the dismantling of internal trade barriers gives foreigners a better opportunity to exploit the common market's enhanced dimension than it gives some of their European competitors, who will have to adapt their strategies to a truly single market and forgo some of the protections they enjoyed in fragmented markets. Another probable consequence of the internal market will be greater competition worldwide with U.S. businesses, but that is a development to be welcomed by those who see competition as a spur to greater economic efficiency.

Rather than resist greater European integration – a positive process that in any case is beyond the capacity of the United States to forestall – it should take up the challenge of dealing with a closer union of the Twelve, urging it down paths congenial to U.S. interests. Many avenues of dialogue already exist between Brussels and Washington. They all are fragmented, which is probably unavoidable. Military questions and security problems are dealt with in the framework of NATO. Economic issues affecting the Western world are discussed in the Organization for Economic Cooperation and Development and during the Western Economic Summits. Financial matters are addressed by the Group of Five, the Group of Seven, the Group of Ten, and so on. Trade and agriculture problems give rise to shouting matches between U.S. administration and Commission representatives, bilaterally or in the GATT.

On neither side of the Atlantic is there a global overview of the complex and rich relationship between the Twelve and the United States. The danger inherent in the absence of such a view is that single issues may dominate the headlines and poison the relationship. Trade frictions and general economic competition are going to be a permanent feature of our relationship in the years ahead. Difficult discussions must take place on the issues of burden sharing, the transfer of military technology, and the common procurement of military equipment. Financial matters will continue to absorb the energies of our governments and bankers for many years to come. Political and economic developments in the Third World as well as in Eastern Europe and the newly industrialized countries – the so-called NICS – will affect us jointly, but might elicit different reactions that could lead to misunderstanding and distrust.

The absence of a well-coordinated dialogue could play into the hands of those who are interested in separating the United States from Europe. They are to be found in the Kremlin to be sure, but also on both sides of the Atlantic. Fortress America and Independent Europe are alluring prospects for many who have not yet grasped that the world is inexorably inching toward interdependence and multipolarity.

In such a context, it becomes not only desirable but also critical to establish a strong, permanent, and multifaceted dialogue between Washington and the Brussels-based institutions. If the present fragmented and poorly coordinated contacts persist, they could lead to a fatal erosion of the alliance through impatience with each other's complaints as well as bickering about specific issues that have not been sufficiently considered.

Relations with the EC: An Elusive Dialogue

As far as the EC proper is concerned (excluding the EPC for the moment), the United States, just as any other country, has to deal with the Commission, the Presidency, and the member states.

Contacts with the European Bureaucracy

U.S. diplomats often complain that it is difficult to do business with the EC and to obtain a response to U.S. preoccupations. When applying to the Commission, these diplomats say that they sometimes are directed to the member states and the Presidency, which in turn refer them back to the Commission. Such cases have certainly occurred, and more frequently than U.S. diplomats would have liked. Some of it is the obvious stalling tactic in response to a U.S. complaint or to a U.S. request for an explanation of an EC decision that does not satisfy Washington. Everyone, including the United States, plays the game, which is nothing extraordinary. But the complaint goes deeper, reflecting a certain impatience at the way the EC conducts its business, coupled with an occasional misperception of its decision-making procedures.

Many ACP countries, as well as countries of the European Free Trade Association (EFTA), are rather good at taking advantage of the EC's procedures to further their own interests and express their preoccupations.[100] Recognizing that their economic well-being is largely shaped by EC decisions, they always try to be well-informed of the various stages of a decision, an effort that certainly does not overtax them. The EC is literally a glass house, and the more confidential ministerial or COREPER discussions are rapidly leaked to the press and interested parties. Anyone wishing to influence the EC can thus easily make their views known in the Commission and in the capitals, especially in the capital of the Presidency.

Most of these countries emphasize a coordinated approach in contrast to what many Europeans experience as official Washington's piecemeal approach to the EC. A good example of this — one frequently mentioned by Europeans — is the U.S. attitude to the negotiations on Spain's accession to the EC. Shortly after the Socialist government was voted into office, EC member states were approached by U.S. diplomats, who expressed anxiety about how the then-stalled accession negotiations might affect the new government's intentions regarding Spain's continued NATO membership. After Spain became an EC member, the EC, which had made substantial agricultural concessions to Spain, was hit by complaints from the U.S. Trade Representative about how EC agricultural preferences might affect U.S. agricultural exports. Europeans were incensed at what they perceived to be U.S. inconsistency, even though the first U.S. demarche showed a good appreciation of the growing links between defense and political integration.

Negotiating with the EC

Negotiating with the EC also is a frustrating exercise for U.S. teams. On important matters such as trade and agriculture, the EC spokesman and negotiator is the Commission, which receives its mandate from the Council and reports to it. The United States thus finds itself negotiating with the Commission but concurrently seeking to influence both the Commission and the Council. This situation is not different from other negotiations except that so many more players and a dozen capitals are involved. The United States attempts to exercise influence through its missions in Brussels and in the capitals of the member states, usually with special attention to the country holding the Presidency. The nature of the issue sometimes leads the United States to play "divide and rule" and to try, not always unsuccessfully, to sow dissent among the member states. In such cases, U.S. diplomats might well prefer not to approach the Presidency and make its life more difficult within the Council. When the stakes become higher, cabinet-level contacts with members of the Commission and the affected ministers are organized.[101]

Europeans often complain that the position taken by the U.S. administration is always subject to modification by the U.S. Congress. Indeed U.S. negotiators have been adept at brandishing the congressional weapon to extract further concessions from their European counterparts. But Europeans have successfully started taking a leaf from the Americans' own book, the Commission being the administration and the Council assuming the role of Congress.

In this kind of situation, the Presidency plays a behind-the-scenes role. It remains in permanent contact with the Commission and gets first-hand briefings from it. It exerts its influence to get the Council to agree on the initial mandate for the Commission, send signals of support for the Commission during the negotiation, and approve the results achieved by the Commission negotiators. In the course of the negotiation, the mandate may have to be adjusted to the realities of a tough horse trade, especially if the member states had difficulty agreeing on it at the time of its adoption. In such cases, the Council occasionally adopts a mandate that does not entirely satisfy the Commission negotiators but that they accept to avoid delaying the start of a negotiation. Adapting a mandate is never an easy task given the varied and often conflicting interests of the member states and given also that the United States usually has a fairly good idea of what these conflicting interests are and how to exploit them.

Cabinet-level Meetings with the Commission

In an attempt to resolve existing frictions jointly, the United States and the Commission hold a meeting every year at the ministerial level, usually in December. U.S. participants include the secretary of state, who is the delegation leader, and a cabinet-level delegation usually made up of his colleagues from the Treasury, Agriculture, and Commerce departments as well as the special trade representative. The corresponding European commissioners are on hand to discuss the main issues during the two-day conference. An experienced Washington observer of U.S.-EC relations and former participant in U.S.-EC meetings, Kenneth Moss, writes: "It is difficult to find major accomplishments from the ministerial [meeting] . . . [It] is mainly a problem-solving endeavor; it does not identify future problems and suggest courses that might prevent or deflate them."[102]

One of the reasons for this justified criticism is the forum itself. As all-important as the Commission is in the process of European integration, the EC is nevertheless bicephalous ("dual-headed"). The absence of the Presidency or the troika from the conference deprives it of an essential element and considerably reduces its potential. Political efficiency suggests that the Council be involved in future meetings with the United States, perhaps with U.S. legislators also present. The contentious issues are technically well-defined in many cases. Solving them requires the political involvement of both the Commission and the Council on the European side. Recent discussions held between the United States and Europe on the Airbus issue are a good example of what ought to be done more frequently. The Commission, sole European negotiator, found it desirable to involve the ministers from the Airbus countries because of the growing political sensitivity of the issue that had – and still might have – the potential of seriously affecting EC-U.S. relations.

Relations with the EPC: An Incomplete Dialogue

On matters of foreign policy, the Presidency, as the spokesperson for the Twelve, has extensive and growing contacts with third countries because of the interest of these countries in developing a good dialogue with the Twelve. At the present time, formal and informal contacts have been established with every European non-EC member through direct bilateral contacts as well as through the Council of Europe, the Strasbourg-based intergovernmental organization to which all free European countries belong.[103] Political exchanges of views are regularly held between the Twelve and the nine other members of the Council of Europe. Mediterranean countries, as well as the Arab League, also are regular EPC contacts because of the EC's extensive network of bilateral agreements covering aid, trade, and financial assistance.

India, China, and Japan all have established formal links with the EPC at regular intervals through meetings of foreign ministers and political directors. The ASEAN countries have done the same, using a different formula; there are regular encounters between both regional entities to discuss the full range of their concerns and policies in matters of mutual interest—economic as well as political. The EC-ACP meetings also offer an occasion to exchange ministerial-level views between the Twelve and their African, Caribbean, and Pacific partners.

In Central America, a substantial overall dialogue has been established between the Twelve and the five concerned Central American countries. The Contadora Group countries have always attended because of their regional peacekeeping potential. The Andean Group has also developed a working relationship with the Twelve, using EC–Andean Group meetings originally conceived to cover EC assistance to the budding regional entity and later expanded to cover political issues.

The content of these dialogues with third countries and regions is usually comprehensive and will normally extend beyond issues of direct mutual interest. The Japanese, for example, have been interested in the INF debate in Europe and exchanged views with the Twelve on this matter. The discussion with them also frequently covered the regions of the world that are of less concern to Tokyo, such as Africa and Latin America, as well as other issues, such as the budgetary problems experienced by the UN.

The purpose of this review of EPC contacts is to contrast it with the relations it has with the United States. Indeed, U.S. contacts with the EPC are remarkably less comprehensive than some the Twelve have with other major international partners, such as China and Japan. In fact, the United States is the only major country with which the EPC maintains such a low level of dialogue, except for the Soviet Union. And even this might change shortly if newly announced Soviet policies are implemented.[104] The effect of intensified contacts between the Twelve and the USSR would be to make the United States odd man out as far as the EPC is concerned. Systematic contacts do take place, of course, but the level is not the same, and the amount of preparation involved, at least on the EPC side, is not as thorough as it is with other countries.

At the start of the Presidency, the foreign minister meets with the U.S. secretary of state and covers with him a range of international problems of mutual interest. He also often takes the opportunity, when in Washington, to confer with congressional leaders and other cabinet officers, such as the secretary of commerce or the special trade representative. The agenda is jointly established by the United States and the Presidency alone; there is no formal EPC preparation for these meetings.

The main differences in U.S. relations, compared with the EPC's contacts with other major third countries, are the presence of the Presidency alone, not the troika; the lack of a mandate for the president, who does not formally speak on behalf of the Twelve; the relative absence of preparation among the Twelve; and the informal character of these meetings, which, although habitual, lack a formal commitment. These are significant differences, which in no way serve to foster a serious political dialogue at the ministerial level.

Contacts are more systematic at the official level. The political director, who leads the troika, meets with his U.S. counterpart. And an endless stream of U.S. officials, mostly from the Department of State, visits their counterparts in the Presidency, and vice versa. Preparations for these meetings are more extensive, and the Presidency always attempts to define a common position for the Twelve on the issues to be discussed with the Americans, although that is not always possible. The Presidency then has to admit that there is no consensus. In most instances, though, the Presidency has a degree of latitude that enables it to present its own national point of view and may discuss the debate within the Twelve without identifying those member states that take different attitudes. The U.S. side generally knows, of course, where the differences lie and what the causes are.

Although not very structured in the early days, these encounters between the political directors of the troika and their Washington counterparts are useful essentially for comparing notes on the gamut of international problems. Their main drawback is the absence of any discussion of the political relations between the participants themselves. The lack of an EPC working group handling relations between the Twelve and the United States reflects the existence of NATO and the web of special relations between each of the Twelve and Washington.

The embassies of the Twelve and the EC mission of the Commission in Washington are also active in this relationship. Regular coordination and information meetings are held in the embassy of the country holding the Presidency. Demarches will be carried out in the name of the Twelve by the ambassador of that country, alone or leading the troika.

Another promising dialogue exists between the U.S. Congress and the European Parliament. Meetings are held alternately in the United States and in the EC. Lawmakers on both sides of the Atlantic thus get regular exposure to the other side's problems and views. Most of them have been happy with the experience and the opportunity it has given them to confront divergent opinions on a broad range of questions.

Reasons for the incomplete dialogue between Washington and Brussels are essentially political. Most European governments have not been willing up to now to pool their experiences in their bilateral relationship with the United States. They do so more readily for questions of mutual interest in other parts of the world, where Europeans and Americans, in addition to discussing the issues, sometimes also try to cooperate with one another to achieve largely common goals. Until recently security played the dominant role, with most European leaders reluctant to engage in discussions concerning their military security outside of the NATO framework. The major European countries also wanted to preserve their "privileged" relationship with their ultimate protector and one of their main markets.

Washington has long given the EPC scant attention. The EPC's credibility has been weak in the United States because it is considered long on talk and short on action. When the EPC started to become more credible, officials in Washington took greater notice, though with patchy enthusiasm. Their minds are still all but exclusively set on the NATO relationship, which they consider the appropriate forum for political questions. Some of them also fear weakening the alliance by recognizing the EPC. Both sides thus share the blame for the present imperfect dialogue. Remedying this deficiency would be in their mutual long-term interest.

Improving the U.S.-EC Dialogue

In recent years, some member states have tried to expand the existing regular exchanges with the United States, especially at the ministerial level, and make them more efficient, less constrained by too rigid an agenda, and more informative. Foreign ministers of the Twelve have raised this issue in at least three of the more recent informal weekend meetings organized by each successive Presidency. The Dutch, British, and Belgian presidencies placed the issue on their agendas for these meetings and achieved a quasi-consensus on the format for the meetings and on the desirability for improvements in general. At that time, the troika was considered the most appropriate vehicle for meetings with the U.S. secretary of state. The lone, hesitant foreign minister had promised to raise the issue with his president and to convey to him the desire of all his colleagues to start a more substantial dialogue with Washington. The succeeding Danish and German presidencies, no doubt absorbed by more immediate issues, have not revived the discussion.

During his visit to Washington in February 1987, Belgian Foreign Minister Léo Tindemans raised the issue with Secretary of State George Shultz. The secretary seemed ready for a systematic dialogue between the United States and the Twelve, especially on major economic issues such as debt and development. According to Secretary Shultz, the United States and the Twelve must devote greater joint attention to the actions of the World Bank, the International Monetary Fund, and the GATT.[105]

The mechanics for such an improved dialogue are not difficult to establish. The experience of the EPC in dealing with many foreign partners suggests that the troika is probably the best vehicle for contacts with the secretary of state, at least for the foreseeable future. Because contacts would also have to be established with other cabinet members, enlarged or specific troikas might be appropriate now and then as long as they are coordinated by the main one. A good example of possible development in this field is the troika run by the ministers responsible for fighting terrorism, which has established contacts with concerned third countries, including the United States.

The presence of the Commission in all troika meetings would ensure continuity as well as full coverage of both EC and EPC issues by the European participants. The U.S. administration would have to organize itself accordingly, with clear leadership probably from the Department of State. At the same time, existing contacts between the Congress and the European Parliament would be developed to parallel the intensified and systematic dialogue by the executives.

No issue should be considered out of bounds. This condition will not be easy to achieve because of some EC members' reluctance to address security issues in the framework of the Twelve. Yet experience has shown that much can still be accomplished. The security issue can continue to be addressed inside NATO—with an active role for the WEU—until such time as Europe will have managed to include defense as an element of its integration process. The existence of an overall dialogue will be beneficial for NATO itself because the security dimension will always be a part of any broadened dialogue – even if it must remain implicit for some time. The number of common issues is so overwhelming, however, that this temporary hurdle need not be an obstacle to a mutually beneficial dialogue.

Most economic and political issues require common analysis, whether they are bilateral U.S.-EC problems that cannot be allowed to grow beyond manageable proportions or international issues demanding joint management. The EC Presidency would have to play a leading role in establishing and developing a dialogue with the United States. It would share this responsibility with the Commission as a European delegation that is bicephalous, a correct reflection of the existing institutional structure of the evolving European integration. The United States will find it in its long-term interest to pay more attention to the Presidency and to start working much more closely with it than it has done in the past.

Clearly, improvements must be made on both sides of the Atlantic. Existing channels should be fully used and better ones set up when needed. Ministerial-level discussions between the troika and the secretary of state would force participants to start considering the EC-U.S. relationship in more global terms. More important, the executive and legislative branches in Washington and the Commission and the Presidency in Brussels must strengthen their efforts to coordinate their policies much more closely with one another than they have done up to now.

10

Where to from Here?

The EC is far more than a group of states with a few important but compartmentalized mutual interests – NATO or the OECD, for example. But it is still not a confederation. It is a condominium of 12 sovereign nations pushing against the fine line between the promise and the price of greater integration.

The rotating Presidency symbolizes the very essence of the EC. Because the Presidency is mainly responsible for the internal coherence and coordination of the activities of the EC councils, the EPC, and the European Council, the presidencies that have not managed to achieve minimum coordination among the various EC councils have not been successful. The much lighter institutional structure of the EPC and the nature of its purpose – deprived of the legislative and regulatory powers of the EC and largely limited to the consideration of policies and the hammering out of policy statements – have made it totally dependent on the Presidency. The European Council is the "crowning touch" in the Presidency's attempts to link EC activities with those of the EPC.

The Presidency acts as spokesperson of the Council and of the EPC. It represents both in the European Parliament, an emerging force that the Presidency and the Commission will have to reckon with far more in the future, thanks to the new provisions of the Single European Act. And in dealing with third countries, the Presidency is the leading contact, sharing that responsibility with the Commission in EC affairs and exercising it alone in matters covered by the EPC.

Beyond the obvious need for someone to manage the Council and provide coherence to its activities, the Presidency's main advantage probably lies in the educational process that accompanies it. As a government prepares to take over from its predecessor, its administration is forced to take a look at the way it operates and to reorganize itself to an extent that varies from country to country, with the smaller countries usually more affected by the process. Public awareness of European integration increases sharply, spotlighting that country's participation and unleashing debates about its place in today's Europe and the influence of integration on its future.[106] Thus forced to pay greater attention to these debates, the government cannot afford to disregard its people's desire for "more Europe."

Some presidencies will be more activist than others; some will take a modest view of their role, while others will set out with more ambitious objectives. National traditions and idiosyncracies are apparent in the way member states approach this function and discharge it. All attempts to unify the basic operational requirements for the successful running of a Presidency have bumped against this obstacle and are likely to continue doing so, at least until compelling reasons force a change.

Because the importance of the Presidency has usually been either downplayed or exaggerated, the right balance has rarely been achieved. Excessively emphasizing the Commission misses the continued relevance of the member states in the decision-making process. Inflated expectations of the Presidency's role downplay the importance of the Commission and of the European Parliament. They also lose sight of the short duration of a presidential mandate, compared with the four-year terms for commissioners or the five-year terms for MEPs. The General Secretariat of the Council offsets this handicap only to a limited extent because its overriding emphasis is on political weight. And that can only make itself felt through duration, precisely the ingredient lacking in the six-month presidential term of office.

Toward European Union

The Twelve have thus evolved a complex structure that some observers compare with the U.S. political machinery and its system of checks and balances. Not yet as complete as the U.S. system, it is still evolving. Innovation will result from dynamic and interactive change in the member states and the outside world. Had the EC also displayed a sense of humor, it might have done well to erect statues to several unobvious, but nonetheless real, cofounders of European integration, such as Joseph Stalin, Japanese microchip and Brazilian textile manufacturers, and Reagan and Gorbachev sitting together in Reykjavik. External shocks have always spurred the EC on, and there is no reason to expect this to change.

European institutions mirror the complexity of the integration endeavor. Integration's logic will lead to reduced powers of the member states and to greater transfer of individual sovereignty to common institutions designed to enhance the sovereignty of all. Arguments about the loss or reduction of sovereignty shed much of their emotional appeal when expressed in terms of enhanced joint sovereignty. European political leaders will have to confront a classical problem of perceptions and symbolism.

The ultimate goal of integration is European Union. Those who believe that the EC will not progress beyond a single integrated market express fashionable cynicism. They also exhibit a lack of appreciation of the long-term trends of history. Why indeed should the nation-state represent the ultimate and definitive stage in the evolution of

Europe since the fall of the Roman Empire? As external pressures have built and forced small entities to coalesce for survival into ever larger ones, thus will it be with the present European nation states that will have to unite to resist domination by other stronger and more competitive entities.

The process, because it is slow, has led to discouragement and impatience in Europe and skepticism abroad. But the pace of life is increasing. Several decades will not pass before European political integration – including a defense component – emerges in a continent exposed to the many demographic, economic, and military pressures of a multipolar world.

Because businesses already operate internationally, controlling the impact of their activities on national interests constitutes a major headache for all governments. The present situation is comparable with that of Europe in the Middle Ages. At the time, Florentine bankers were weaving their web beyond the borders of their small feudal principalities. The scope of today's operations dwarfs that of the Florentines, but the basic trends are similar.

Changes will be implemented gradually, as new conditions and needs are perceived. The Presidency will no doubt be affected by these changes. To what extent is hard to forecast in the short term, though some suggestions will be made later. In the long term, the Council should gradually transform itself into an upper house elected by the national parliaments. It would have a role comparable to that of the U.S. Senate or the German Bundesrat in defending the interest of the member states. The directly elected European Parliament would then become the lower house, exercising the traditional control and budgetary powers. Legislative work would be shared by both houses.

The Commission, when suitably adapted, would turn itself into a true executive, responsible before both houses of Parliament. Its size would have to be reduced; the presence of at least one member from each of the member states would no longer be required because the Commission would be controlled by a reinforced Parliament. The Commission's president would be directly elected by all Europeans to symbolize Europe's identity.[107]

None of these long-term perspectives are likely to come about before the next century — although it might be useful not to forget the irony of Bismarck's privately mourning, as late as 1869, that he would not live to see the German Empire, which emerged the very next year when the combined armies of the German states defeated Napoleon III.

Between the Present and the Future

Clearly, the Presidency is going to be around for some time in its present form. Is its role likely to increase? Contradictory trends make an answer difficult to shape in terms of clear options. On the one hand, the present Commission has used its powers much more aggressively and reversed the declining fortunes of some of its predecessors. The Presidency had taken on additional roles because earlier Commissions had been timid in using the full scope of their powers; a reversal in this trend could bring about a relative decline of the Presidency's influence.

Increased EC membership has also strengthened the Commission's hand, because 12 member states only exercise presidential responsibilities once every six years for a limited period of six months and with different approaches and skills. This could further weaken the Presidency to the benefit of the Commission and the Parliament.

Some member states are also impatient with the limited potential of the EPC to progress substantially because of unanimity requirements and repeated presidential changes. Indeed, the troika notwithstanding, the policies adopted by previous presidencies can be ruined by the failure of a succeeding Presidency to press on with the same policies. At the present, no one can force a reluctant president to do more than go through the motions. These limiting factors are thus likely to strengthen the push toward greater reliance on common institutions to project Europe's role in the world. Changes in the Soviet Union and in the relationship between the two superpowers will in all likelihood accelerate this trend.

On the other hand, nationalism is still flourishing in Europe. Integration causes deep resentment and fear, conscious or not, among a sizable number of politicians and bureaucrats who rightly perceive it as a threat to their powers and prerogatives. The Council is the place in which these politicians and bureaucrats can make their power felt, by slowing down or killing Commission proposals. Future presidencies must thus expect rearguard actions, some of which will be successful.

In such a context, third countries will have to keep dealing with both the Commission and the Presidency for many years to come. Failure to do so will give rise to misunderstandings and inefficiencies. Third countries may not prefer an institutional setup as complex, but it is the only one the Europeans have managed to develop without recourse to the coercion used in previous unification attempts of the nineteenth and twentieth centuries. Slow by everyday standards, European integration has been moving along rapidly when measured against the time scale of history. Its relative slowness is a powerful guarantee that its peoples will remain committed to the process that they wish to see accomplished at greater speed. Balancing these two contradictory timings has been — and will remain — a permanent feature of the EC's development, to the occasional discomfort of third countries.

What improvements could bolster the efficiency of the Presidency and the Council? Much as been written about this, mostly in internal documents of the EC. Several of them will have to be looked at again as politicians and bureaucrats grapple with an evolving Community in an evolving world. The present wide array of separate councils can only continue to exist without causing serious breakdowns if it meets at least one and preferably two conditions. Foremost is the requirement that national governments make a much greater effort to coordinate their positions in the various councils and to impose a common discipline on their representatives. This requirement is valid for all member states. The worst offenders usually are not the least integrationist.[108] In addition, one of the councils must be mandated to make a final decision in the event that separate councils reach differing conclusions on the same issue or, as is often the case, differences between councils preclude any decision from being made.

A much-discussed formula has been the return to a single Council. Meeting more frequently than once a month, its members would be European ministers appointed in each capital for this purpose. Responsible for an overall coordinated approach, the ministers would be assisted by other cabinet members according to the issues on the Council's agenda. This appealing solution may raise more problems than it would solve, however. The European minister could become a superminister, more powerful than his national colleagues and a potential threat to his prime minister because of the growing reach of the European factor in all facets of domestic and international policy. Or he could come to depend on the goodwill of some of his colleagues, who would dictate the positions to be defended by him in Brussels and in addition find him a convenient go-between, allowing them to escape direct confrontation with their European counterparts on tricky issues where their national policies would isolate them.

Another possible improvement for future presidencies is a more systematic use of majority voting in the Council. The new provisions of the Single European Act offer enough scope for resourceful presidencies to increase dramatically the routine use of majority voting.

As far as the EPC is concerned, a more imaginative use of the troika could help alleviate the Presidency's burden, especially by putting into practice the never-used clause that provides for specific tasks to be delegated by the Presidency to other member states. A preference ought to be given to troika members who could thus ensure a greater degree of continuity and personal commitment. If successful, this approach could be widened to include other presidential tasks, thereby softening the inconveniently short duration of the presidential duties. Voting will also have to be introduced into external relations, and the EPC should gradually align itself with EC practice as integration moves along.[109]

Following the same logic of growing integration on the external front, the EC's representation at the Economic Summits should be borne by the Presidency and the Commission alone, thus doing away with the present unsatisfactory, hybrid formula. Again, this change will have to be introduced gradually. Decision making by majority vote is a crucial issue. If the EC wishes to avoid falling into the vicious circle of enlarged membership causing ever greater dilution, there is no alternative to majority voting short of setting up a two-speed system that would allow the more integration-minded member states to travel faster toward the goal. The political implications of such a step have not been fully weighed, but this step has been seriously contemplated in the past and could crop up again.

All of these suggested improvements pave the way for the gradual transformation of the Council into the powerful Senate envisioned in the previous section. Voting is the essence of a legislative body. Specialized councils are the basis of future senate committees. Reconciling differing points of view is a function of the many coordinating bodies of any assembly; the ultimate arbiter is the plenary session. The permanent presence of the Commission in the troika will smooth the transfer to it of executive responsibilities for foreign policy. The Council in its future guise as European Senate is required to advise and consent, a familiar expression to Americans that brings up the issue of U.S.-EC relations.

U.S.-EC Relations

The crucial consideration then for the United States should be that the EC is an evolving condominium of friendly states sharing American values. Their strength through cohesion is Western strength. The EC is not coextensive with NATO in Europe and has a merely embryonic security dimension, but its developing unity and prosperity make the Atlantic Alliance more credible.

The United States should encourage, not resist, the political and economic integration of Western Europe. In practice, it has consistently done so since World War II, but it has at times also been ambiguous about it. As a superpower and global trader, the United States has a constant need to push the Twelve, whether individually or as a group, in directions with which they do not feel comfortable. Will the rotating Presidency – in its present and future forms – be an asset or a liability to U.S. diplomacy? That is a question that U.S. policymakers and officials will have to answer. But on balance, the Presidency can be helpful to U.S. interests if it is handled with intelligent delicacy. The EC is a complex organization that presents many open faces to the outside world. It is an unparalleled adventure for the national bureaucracies in managing what is, in effect, a global superpower in the making.

In that process, it is fair to say that the Europeans are refining the art of government and bringing it to a new plateau of sophistication. The EC is an unprecedented exercise in the surrender of sovereignty to a larger whole (at least since 1776), and it has worked pretty well. It also works toward the same fundamental goals as the United States because it shares the same basic values.

U.S. political leaders and officials should thus address all of these varied EC facets with a view toward developing practical and close relations between both shores of our common ocean. At stake is the commonality of purpose and joint effectiveness of a rejuvenated Atlantic Community – a community that will address other values and issues beyond its own self-defense.

Appendix

The EPC Structure

1. *European Council*

   * gathers *once* during the six months of the Presidency;

   * is composed of 11 prime ministers, the president of France, and the president of the EC Commission, all of whom are accompanied by their foreign ministers;

   * coordinates both the EPC and EC;

   * sets out the main political guidelines.

2. *Ministerial Meetings*

   * convene a minimum of *two* times during the six months of the Presidency;

   * occur more frequently through informal meetings and other occasions;

   * are composed of the foreign ministers and a member of the EC Commission;

- function as the main decision-making bodies of the EPC.

3. *Political Committee (POCO)*

   - gathers at least once a month;

   - is composed of the political directors and a senior Commission civil servant;

   - serves as the linchpin of the EPC.

4. *Twenty Working Groups*

   - gather at least once during a Presidency period; frequency depends on the importance of the subjects as well as on international events;

   - are composed of department heads and a Commission representative;

   - serve as the workhorses of EPC;

   - include a special group – the correspondents.

5. *Other Mechanisms*

   - The *European Parliament* has monthly question time, special debates, meetings with the political commission;

   - the *Secretariat* is a newly established, exclusive instrument of the Presidency; participation by diplomats from the member countries rotates;

   - *missions* in the member states as well as in third countries promote cooperation;

   - the *COREU Network* is a special telex link open 24 hours a day.

Notes

1. The original six were Belgium, Germany, France, Italy, Luxembourg, and the Netherlands. Denmark, Ireland, and the UK joined in 1973. Greece became a member in 1981, Spain and Portugal in 1986. Turkey formally applied for membership in 1987. And Austria and Norway are showing interest, a renewal in the case of Norway, which very nearly joined in 1973. Morocco also sent a letter of application, which was discussed by the EC Council of Ministers in Copenhagen on July 13, 1987; the Council concluded that, because it is not a European country, Morocco did not qualify.

2. Many calls for monetary union have been issued since the WERNER plan for economic and monetary union (in 1981). The present European Monetary System (EMS) is an incomplete endeavor toward that end. Basically successful in maintaining exchange rates stability among member countries, it has also given birth to the European Currency Unit (ECU), which has gained limited but growing acceptance as a unit of account and in the Eurobond markets. Belgium issued the first ECU coins, a gold and a silver one, in 1987.

The ECU still suffers from many handicaps, however, such as the limited participation of the pound sterling, the extended fluctuation rates authorized for the Italian lira, German Central Bank reluctance, the absence of a European Central Bank to manage it, and the persistence of some controls of capital movements across the borders. This last handicap is about to disappear. The Germans have strongly hinted that they might become more amenable to the ECU. And French Prime Minister Jacques Chirac, as well as his Finance Minister Edouard Balladur, issued calls in January 1988 to start examining "the possibility of creating a European Central Bank which would manage a Common Currency, the ECU" (*Financial Times*, January 8, 1988).

German reactions to this proposal have ranged from the traditionally negative ones, based on the incomplete state of economic integration and issued by German Chancellor Helmut Kohl and the Bundesbank leadership, to the more positive view of Foreign Minister Hans-Dietrich Genscher. On January 19, the Action Committee for Europe, "The Club of Leading Political and Economic Figures in the 12 Countries of the European Community" (Ian Davison, in the *Financial Times*), strongly supported the French approach.

3. Jean Monnet, *Mémoires* (Paris: Fayard, 1976).

4. See Bertrand de Jouvenel, "Journal du pouvoir (1943)," in *Commentaire*, no. 38 (Summer 1987), published in Paris by Julliard. There is, of course, a very long list of writings on this subject.

5. Two each from Germany, Spain, France, Italy, and the UK, and one each from the remaining seven member states. This number is generally considered too high. Attempts were made before the Spanish and Portuguese accessions to limit them to one per member state, or even less than that, but this fell afoul of problems of internal politics in some of the larger member states — especially Germany at that time — who have the habit of sending to Brussels one commissioner from the ranks of the government majority and one from the opposition.

6. See article 157 of the EEC Treaty.

7. Belgium — Jean Rey; Germany — Walter Hallstein, the first president; France — François-Xavier Ortoli and the current president, Jacques Delors; Italy — Franco-Maria Malfatti; Luxembourg — Gaston Thorn; Netherlands — Sicco Mansholt; United Kingdom — Roy Jenkins.

8. See *L'Acte unique européen*, Commentaire by Jean De Ruyt (Brussels: Editions de l'Université Libre de Bruxelles, 1987), 7.

9. See articles 145 to 153 of the EEC Treaty as amended by the Single European Act. The reader interested in knowing more about EC legislation and its applicability, direct or indirect, spe-

cific or general, will have to refer to article 189 of the EEC Treaty, article 14 of the Paris Treaty, article 161 of the EURATOM Treaty, and the very abundant specialized literature that they have spawned. The decisions of the European Court of Justice are also essential reading.

10. In the case of qualified majority voting, member states' votes are weighted as follows: 10 votes – Germany, France, Italy, United Kingdom; 8 votes – Spain; 5 votes – Belgium, Greece, the Netherlands, Portugal; 3 votes – Denmark, Ireland; 2 votes – Luxembourg. Fifty-four votes are required to achieve a qualified majority. Twenty-three votes thus constitute a blocking minority.

11. See article 6 of the Single European Act.

12. In 1965, a crisis erupted within the EEC. France refused to agree to the full logic of integration and tried to negate some of the provisions for majority voting. French President Charles de Gaulle wished to put a stop to what he saw as a dangerously irreversible trend toward more supranationalism. Disagreement reached the point that France no longer attended Council meetings between July 1965 and January 1966. The French presidential election campaign of December 1965 revealed French public opinion to be divided on this issue, and, in contrast to his first election, de Gaulle had to wait for the second ballot to be reelected.

A compromise was then struck in January 1966. France and its five partners agreed to disagree on the basic question of majority voting. Known as the "Luxembourg Compromise," this agreement states that whenever important interests are at stake, the Council will try to reach a decision acceptable by all. The French added that, in their view, discussion of very important interests had to be pursued until a unanimous agreement emerged. The other delegations did not share this view.

The issue has never been satisfactorily resolved. The "Luxembourg Compromise" in effect hampered the work of the Council, which hardly voted any more. The UK joined the EEC thereafter, specifically referring to the "Luxembourg Compromise" as existing EC practice. The practice in recent years, however, shows that the Council has surmounted its inhibitions and is now voting more and more frequently. Pragmatism and common sense seem to be prevailing and will probably continue to do so unless someone comes up with the urge to reopen the theoretical debate and to cause another round of frustrating and useless discussions.

13. See article 138, paragraph 3, of the EEC Treaty.

14. Examples can be found in Belgium and Germany, and this is being contemplated in other national parliaments. The British Parliament and the Danish Folketing have long had special committees to follow European activities but they draw only on their members, not on MEPs. Their intent is also clearly to control as much as possible any European encroachment on their sovereign powers.

15. See article 7 of the Single European Act, which replaces article 149 of the EEC Treaty and provides for a measure of "codecision" that really grants Parliament a second reading and a far greater influence over what remains a decision made solely by the Council. Opinions vary as to the true meaning of this reform. Parliament itself will be largely responsible for any significant increase in its influence through the skillful use of the new provisions. Because the provisions have only been in effect since July 1, 1987, no definitive judgment can yet be passed.

16. See article 144 of the EEC Treaty.

17. See articles 164 to 188 of the EEC Treaty as amended by articles 11 and 12 of the Single European Act.

18. See articles 4, 5, 11, 12, 26, and 27 of the Single European Act. Also article 18, paragraph 4.

19. See articles 193 to 198 of the EEC Treaty.

20. See articles 146 and 147 of the EEC Treaty as amended by the 1965 Treaty that set up a single Council and a Single Commission for the three European Communities (coal and steel, EEC, and EURATOM).

21. The EC tends to consider that a civilized way of doing business consists in taking holidays during the month of August. That the Southern Hemisphere and the Tropics do not follow that schedule is considered irrelevant. Woe to anyone who tries to transact business with the EC during that period. There is a lone commissioner on duty with a skeleton staff in the nearly empty, labyrinthian Berlaymont building. The Council building is shut. One or two junior diplomats are on hand in the permanent missions of the member states in Brussels. The Presidency usually makes an effort and keeps a few additional staff on duty. The rationale for this nearly complete stop is not only the understandable wish for a break from the usually long working hours. It is

mainly due to the multinational character of the people working for the EC and to their desire to spend some time at home, to avoid becoming rootless Eurocrats.

22. The variety of European traditions also appears in the titles of these junior ministers. In the UK, they are known as a minister or minister of state, the foreign minister being called the foreign secretary and addressed as "minister." In many continental countries, the junior minister will be known as a secretary of state (*secrétaire d'état, secretario de estado, Staatsekretaris*), but delegate minister (*ministre delégué*) or alternate minister has also been used at times. Fortunately, things are not as complicated as they appear. One just has to keep in mind who is the senior minister and address them all as "minister."

23. See article 138, paragraph 3, of the EEC Treaty.

24. Belgian Agriculture Minister and Secretary of State for European Affairs Paul De Keersmaeker was in the chair. Successive Belgian governments always showed strong opposition to what they refer to as the so-called Luxembourg Compromise.

25. For a good view on the topics raised at the Western Economic Summits since their beginnings, see *Economic Summits 1975-1986*, Istituto Affari Internazionali (Rome), ed. (Venice: Fondazione Cini, Isola San Giorgio, 1987), published on the occasion of the 1987 Venice Economic Summit.

26. Ibid., pp. 150-151. Of the 18 issues identified, only four do not fall within EEC competence. They are East-West security (which is addressed by EPC), refugees (indirectly related because of aid issues), regional security, and terrorism (addressed by the Twelve in other forums).

27. They are Danish, Dutch, English, French, German, Greek, Italian, Spanish, and Portuguese.

28. A pregnant issue in recent European Common Market deliberations has been the gender that should be assigned in European languages to the EC monetary unit – the European currency unit or ECU. The Germans are calling it "die ECU" (feminine), while the French favor l'ECU (masculine). Purists (or perhaps male chauvinists) suspect that the distinction is meaningful. A feminine ECU may be considered merely as a unit of account, but a masculine ECU could someday become a real EC currency. The EC Commission, uncertain of the ECU's future, took a middle ground. It denied that gender prejudges the EC's destiny and left it to the member countries to choose their preferred usage. The

British, taking the bull by the horns, will probably go for "the ECU."

29. The European Council held on February 11-13, 1988 adopted three significant measures that strengthened budgetary discipline in agriculture; introduced agricultural stabilizers to set annual guarantee thresholds for cereals, oilseeds, and protein products (in addition to the already existing ones for milk production); and provided financial aids for the early retirement of farmers.

30. Ibid.

31. When one considers the frequency of EC ministerial meetings and adds the informal and EPC meetings, it becomes evident that the ministers know one another's personal strengths and weaknesses fairly well.

32. Little basic literature is available on the EPC. The chief reference work so far is Philippe de Schoutheete, *La coopération politique européene*, 2nd rev. ed. (Brussels: Ed. Labor, 1986). An English language version is in the offing. The same author is about to publish a paper called "The Presidency and the Management of Political Cooperation" as a separate chapter in a forthcoming book (fall 1988), *European Political Cooperation in the 1980s* (Leiden: Martinus Nijhoff).

The German Auswaertiges Amt. regularly publishes an English language version of the more recent basic European texts, *European Political Cooperation (EPC)*, 4th ed. (Bonn: Press and Information Office of the Federal Government, 1982). In 1974, the British Foreign and Commonwealth Office published a useful brochure, "European Political Cooperation: Basic Texts," which is somewhat dated. Many other authors discuss the EPC of course, but always as a part of more general works. See especially Colm O. Nuallain and Jean-Marc Hoscheit, eds., *The Presidency of the European Council of Ministers* (London: Croom Helm, 1985), with special attention to chapters 1 and 12 by Dr. Helen Wallace. This book presents the various ways in which the different member states carry out the Presidency functions.

33. See article 30 of the Single European Act.

34. See the Luxembourg Report, part one, paragraph 7.

35. Final communiqué of the conference of heads of state or government in The Hague, December 2, 1969.

36. Ibid., part two, paragraph 1.

37. Ibid., part two, paragraph 4.

38. A full account of its progress falls outside the scope of this paper. See the reference work mentioned in note 32.

39. All of the texts of these documents are brought together in an instruction book aptly named *Coutumier*, which expands as new instructions are issued by the ministers or the political directors. Finding one's way through the maze of instructions piled upon one another much in the manner that common law developed has become a virtuoso exercise for diplomatic initiates.

40. Before the Single European Act established the secretariat in Brussels, all the working groups met in the capital of the country holding the Presidency. This was quite popular with the participants because it entailed traveling to pleasant cities. As far as the host country was concerned, it was a major organizational challenge and a source of considerable traveling expenses that added to the burden of running the Presidency. Most people thus welcomed the secretariat as a means of relieving them of the burden of organizing the meetings; they also welcomed the decision to concentrate all of the meetings in a single spot well-equipped to handle them. The only net losers turned out to be the Belgian diplomats who no longer got to travel anywhere, although the general secretary of the Belgian Foreign Ministry was happy with the savings in his budget.

41. The place of the Commission in the EPC is now well established. At the beginning, though, it was merely tolerated by some member states who saw no need for regular Commission participation. As the EPC developed, a permanent need for the Commission to be a full participant became more and more apparent. Apart from the information it obtained on international political problems, it helped the member states avoid taking positions that might have contradicted what they were saying as a Community in other international forums. In addition, the EPC and the EC complement and need one another. Commission proposals introduced in the Council cannot ignore the basic political orientations of the EPC, and the EPC in turn cannot disregard the extensive external exposure of the EC.

42. See Schoutheete, *La coopération politique européene*, 40. Author's translation from the French text.

43. For these weekend get-togethers, the foreign ministers and one member of the Commission – usually the president or the commissioner in charge of external relations – are each accompa-

nied by one aide for liaison purposes, but they are alone in their intimate meeting room. Presidencies make a great effort at housing them in comfortable and prestigious accommodations. As Europe abounds with historical buildings, it is not too difficult to find a chateau or an old abbey with all the modern amenities. Security is very tight, and no press is allowed anywhere near the grounds. The object of these meetings is to give ministers an opportunity to air their views in a relaxed and congenial atmosphere without the usual external pressures. Needless to say, they also get to know one another far better.

The habit of inviting spouses to accompany them has taken hold recently. Although there is a separate spouses' program during the day, their presence impedes ministers from having their usual shirtsleeve dinners, which may not be a welcome development as far as efficiency is concerned. On the other hand, ministers are so often away on weekends that some of them welcome the opportunity to see their spouses a bit more often. Spouses also get to know one another, as well as their husbands' colleagues, which reinforces the sense of belonging to a club.

44. This format in effect gives the Commission a privileged position because it is the only permanent troika member; the other members rotate. Its privilege must be viewed, however, in the context of the Commission's overall participation in EPC. It takes part in the discussion but not in the decision; that is left to the partner states.

There have been multiple variations according to the time, place, and quality of the opposite numbers and the availability of potential participants—for example, three ministers, three ambassadors, three political directors, one minister plus two ambassadors, or one ambassador and one political director, and so on.

45. At least that is what is foreseen by the EPC standard operating procedures. In practice, compliance is good and the local Foreign Ministry organizes briefings for the partners' embassies fairly shortly after the visit has taken place. Some capitals are better at this than others, sometimes owing to design but mostly to better organization or more numerous personnel. Briefings are considered useful by most officials and appreciated by local embassies who thus see their role in another member state's capital, if not enhanced, at least not diminished by the EPC. The briefings complement the information circulated by COREU or given during the various EPC meetings.

46. Usually under the form of a dinner or lunch hosted by the ambassador of the country holding the Presidency.

47. In third countries, the term "missions" also embraces the local Commission delegations. The meetings of the Twelve in Washington thus always include a member of the Commission's delegation. Special provisions exist for the many countries in which all of the Twelve are not represented, as is often the case. It is thus common practice, say, for the Italian embassy to act on behalf of the Irish Presidency. Instructions will then be issued by Rome upon the request of Dublin. The three Benelux countries have a special set of agreements whereby Luxembourg is represented by the Netherlands for political matters – and thus for EPC affairs – and by Belgium for economic and trade matters – and thus for EC affairs.

48. In their June 1983 *Solemn Declaration on European Union*, the heads of state and government prescribed "a closer cooperation between the missions of the Ten [as they then were] on diplomatic and administrative matters" (translation by the author from the French text). POCO implemented this by issuing the following instructions to identify the areas of cooperation proposed to the missions in third countries: exchange of political and economic information, common information on administrative problems, mutual assistance in the use of facilities (such as meeting rooms, telecommunications, and other logistical problems), drafting of common contingency plans in cases of crisis, common security measures, cooperation on consular matters, cooperation on health matters, cooperation in the fields of information and culture, and cooperation on development aid. Although these have been issued as general guidelines that are not appropriate for every capital, they are a useful reference for the ambassador entrusted with a six-month's term of presidential responsibility on the spot. Note that the Commission's offices abroad are included in this scheme.

49. See article 30, paragraph 10g, of the Single European Act.

50. Ibid.

51. In the matter of linguistics, the Germans have been more intransigent than the others. They have managed to obtain a modification of the current EPC practice in the text of the Single European Act, which now states that the linguistic regime of the EC will henceforth be applicable to the EPC – i.e., that all lan-

guages are on the same footing. That new general rule is notably tempered, however, by the following sentence in the new text indicating that EPC's current practice will be retained for meetings held below the ministerial level as well as for the COREU traffic.

At their informal "Gymnich" meetings, ministers make a point of speaking either French or English, except when they do not have a sufficient command of either one or they insist on speaking German. Whispered translation is on hand – sometimes courtesy of an expert diplomat, whose usual function is not that of providing translation and who presumably can be relied upon to take copious notes and give advice to his minister, if requested. Even though it is undeniably an advantage of the EPC, compared with EC practice, to have its business conducted only in two languages, diplomats who are not either English or French native speakers are at a disadvantage to their colleagues. This is generally true, however well most of them manage to dominate foreign languages. It is especially apparent in the COREU messages where one finds occasional Germanisms or Hispanisms. It is up to the English and French native speakers then to adapt to these situations with the required tact and admiration for their colleagues' overall linguistic abilities. This explains why strictly adhering to the rule of the COREU system forbids the use of abbreviations or acronyms that are not in general use. Difficult enough to understand, sometimes even for native speakers, these would become totally obscure to the others.

52. See Philippe de Schoutheete's forthcoming chapter mentioned in note 32.

53. See note 39.

54. Two fairly recent examples of a majority being frustrated by the opposition of a single partner are the Korean airliner incident and the attempt to renew normal diplomatic contacts with Syria. In the first instance, the Twelve were prevented from condemning the Soviet Union because of the stubborn opposition of one member state, Greece, which also held the presidency. The meeting became so heated that several foreign ministers were restrained from leaving Athens prematurely with the greatest difficulty. One bulky minister appeared to want to get up and strike his presiding colleague, who was the stubborn one. He eventually refrained from doing so, not without uttering several choice expletives.

In the second case, one country refused to allow the Presidency during the first six months of 1987 to reestablish the contacts with Syria that had been broken off by the Twelve as a consequence of the proven Syrian attempt to blow up an Israeli airliner after takeoff from London. Recognition by all the other partners that Syria had made some conciliatory gestures and that the situation in the Middle East required the involvement of Damascus for any progress toward settling the region's many problems did not sway that one delegation. Contacts were resumed six months later under the subsequent Presidency.

During the preparatory phase of the Single European Act, the European Council had established a special committee under the chairmanship of the Irish senator James Dooge. Supposedly modeled after the Spaak Committee that was decisive in getting the Rome treaties off the ground, the Dooge Committee also tackled the majority problem faced by the EPC, but without achieving consensus. During the negotiations leading to the Single European Act, an attempt was made, which very nearly succeeded, to get the member states to agree not to block a majority view when in a minority of one on a question not vital to one's interests (in effect agreeing to abstain). In the end, this proved to be too much for some of the more traditional defenders of national sovereignty in the narrow sense.

55. Every European state literally means that. Lichtenstein is a participant, and the Vatican has observer status. Given the numbers and the balance of interests, three groups have emerged—the Western group (NATO plus Ireland through its EPC membership), the Eastern group (the Warsaw Pact countries), and all the others clustered under the uncertain banner of the Neutral and Non-Aligned (NNA) group.

56. Excerpted from the statement made by Aldo Moro on the occasion of the signature of the Helsinki Final Act on July 30, 1975 (translation by the author from the French text of Mr. Moro's declaration).

57. Ireland never imposed sanctions for reasons connected with the Northern Ireland situation. Italy went along only briefly because of the large size of the Italian ethnic group in the Argentinian population.

58. The EPC has established a working group to deal with the political aspects of terrorism. It works in close cooperation with the TREVI groups in which police and counterterrorism specialists deal with the more immediately operational aspects of

the fight against it. A substantial measure of cooperation between both has been achieved. Foreign ministers and their colleagues in charge of the special services have mutually benefited from the cross-feed between these two groups.

59. The 12 foreign ministers had agreed at the London European Council in December 1986 to spend the whole of their meeting in the following February discussing the Middle East in the wake of the Irangate affair. As he took over the Presidency, Belgian foreign minister Léo Tindemans was determined that Europe's voice be heard, especially at a time when Washington was paralyzed because of the Irangate scandal. POCO carefully prepared its recommendations to the ministers. Extensive consultations with all interested parties were carried out to ascertain whether the Twelve could do anything significant in the search for a solution in these intertwined, long-lasting conflicts.

The Twelve reached the unanimous conclusion that an international conference on the Middle East would probably offer a credible way out of the present and dangerous stalemate. Many Arab leaders had expressed the hope that Europe would indeed speak out, as it did in 1980 with its Venice Declaration, which recognized the right both of Israel to exist in security and of the Palestinians to exercise their legitimate rights. Israelis were already divided then between the conflicting views of Shimon Peres and Yitzhak Shamir, who jointly headed an uneasy coalition.

The main elements of the declaration, adopted on February 23, 1987 and known as the Brussels Declaration on the Middle East, are as follows:

- The Twelve begin by restating their close and important ties with the region, whose proximity does not allow them to remain passive in the face of developments there that can affect them.
- They restate their conviction that the search for peace in the region remains "a fundamental objective."
- They express their interest in the search for negotiated solutions to reestablish a lasting peace, good neighbor relations, and economic and social development. In so doing they recall their Venice Declaration.
- They then declare themselves in favor of an International Peace Conference under the aegis of the United Nations and with the participation of interested parties (not otherwise defined so as to leave open all formulas for the repre-

sentation of the Palestinians) as well as of parties (not otherwise defined so as to leave an opening for possible Soviet participation, seen as necessary, especially in the light of the relations between Moscow and Damascus at that time) in a position to contribute to the establishment of peace and security in the region and to its economic and social development. This conference, in their opinion, should constitute an appropriate framework for direct negotiations between interested parties.

- The Twelve state their readiness to play a role in this conference and to contribute, either through the Presidency or individually, to narrow the differences between the parties.
- They end with a call for the improvement to the populations of the occupied territories' living standards and a recall of the EC's decisions to afford them economic aid as well as preferential access to the common market.

60. The British, French, and Italian navies took part in the August 1984 Suez Canal operation. The Dutch had expressed their readiness to join them, but the operation was successfully completed before they could do so. Five navies of WEU member countries are in the Gulf. They are present with mine-countermeasure vessels as well as with other surface combatants. Belgium, France, Italy, the Netherlands, and the United Kingdom all operate there in close coordination with one another as well as with the United States.

61. See Kenneth Moss, "The European Community and Transatlantic Relations," in the *Washington Quarterly* 11, no. 1 (Spring 1988) (Washington, D.C.: Center for Strategic and International Studies). The article is one of the most thoughtful and appropriate recent publications on U.S. attitudes toward the EC.

62. See Léo Tindemans, "European Union," report to the European Council, chapter II.C.3, December 1975. Published by the EC Commission in its *Bulletin of the European Communities*, supplement of January 1976.

63. See the following: The *Copenhagen Document on the European Identity*, December 14, 1973; Tindemans, "European Union"; the *London Report*, 1981, prepared for the EPC and adopted by the foreign ministers; *Solemn Declaration on European Union*, June 19, 1983, adopted at Stuttgart by the European Council; *Treaty of European Union*, the draft text adopted in 1984

by the European Parliament; the final report of the Ad Hoc Committee for Institutional Problems, addressed to the June 1985 Milan European Council; and the text of the Single European Act adopted in 1986.

64. The current president of the Commission is the former French finance minister Jacques Delors, who gave his name to the plan to implement the internal market by the end of 1992. The senior vice president is Lorenzo Natali of Italy. Delors is a moderate Socialist and Natali is a Christian Democrat. Both men's mandates expire at the end of 1988. The June 1988 European Council has taken the decision to renew Delors's mandate for another two years.

65. Until the 1985 legislative elections, this did not present much of a problem because all three men were of the same party. But the advent of *la coexistence* – known in many other European countries simply as coalition government – changed this and introduced some noticeable tensions in the composition of the French delegations, especially in the early days of this new formula. Prime Minister Chirac insisted in coming, too, because of the political situation in France and his past involvement in European affairs when he was agriculture minister. The result has been to relegate the foreign minister somewhat. Since the 1988 legislative elections, all three are again of the same party.

66. The European Council usually starts with lunch on the first day – in most instances, but not always, a Monday – and ends after lunch on the following day. Exceptions have been numerous though, either because it quickly became apparent that the meeting was not going anywhere or, more often, because discussions require more time. Prime ministers met nearly all night on the second day of the Luxembourg meeting that led to the Single European Act, and they did so again in their February 1988 meeting that saw the adoption of a comprehensive set of measures destined to prepare the EC for the 1992 deadline.

67. Belgium staved off an impending political crisis – over language problems – during the first six months of the year, thanks to the skillful use by Prime Minister Wilfried Martens of the argument of the EC Presidency. His government fell in the autumn. Denmark, holding the Presidency in the second half of 1987, held elections during that period, but did not form a new government until the one in office had finished discharging its presidential responsibilities.

68. The first summits were Gaullian summonses. Prime Minister de Gaulle called two meetings in 1961 to explain his political ideas to his colleagues. The impact was presumably so strong that they did not repeat the experience until 1967, when they met in Rome to commemorate the tenth anniversary of the treaties. The 1969 summit, held in The Hague, paved the way for British membership. Three summits were then held, one each in the years 1972 to 1974, when it was decided to establish the European Council.

69. At that Council, which successfully decided to establish an intergovernmental conference to modify the Treaty of Rome and thus laid the groundwork for the Single European Act, the French persuaded the Germans to jointly table a draft proposal establishing the European Council as the single decision-making body for both the EPC and the EC under the name of the Council of the European Union. A Secretariat General of this Council, based in Brussels, would also be established. This proposal was greeted with considerable dismay by the Italians and the Benelux countries because it meant that the EC Commission would in effect become subordinate to the newly established structure, thus doing away at one stroke with the supranational element of the EC structure. Many also felt that this proposal skirted the debate about the future European Union, which would have been declared in existence without any of the qualitative improvements desired by the partisans of a stronger and more integrated Europe. Such a proposal was in line with French ideas concerning a presidential approach to Europe. Both former President Giscard and President Mitterrand publicly entertained the notion of "a president for Europe," obviously implying that the president would be a Frenchman – and why not Giscard or Mitterrand himself?

70. See the Parliament's draft text, *Treaty of European Union*, adopted in 1984. Though indeed going beyond what was deemed possible at the time by most informed participants in the work of integration, the Parliament's text proved to contain useful suggestions and, above all, to have reawakened public opinions to some extent, thus putting pressure on the governments. The Single European Act, succeeding where the *Solemn Declaration on European Union* failed, came about in part because of Parliament's prodding.

71. See the *Solemn Declaration on European Union*, paragraph 2.1.2.

72. See article 2 of the Single European Act.

73. Ibid.

74. Depending upon the expectations stemming from the agenda topics, the press contingent will hover between 600 and more than 1,000 accredited journalists, camera crews, etc. The majority comes from the 12 member states and the large press corps permanently covering the EC activities from Brussels. The number of really "foreign" journalists–those from outside the EC–varies depending on the international issues taking front-page prominence at the time and the topics likely to be raised.

Although usually held in a capital city, the European Council has frequently met in other cities, depending upon internal politics. Recent examples have been the 1979 meeting in Strasbourg with the French emphasizing the European dimension of the city, the 1983 and 1987 meetings in Stuttgart and Hamburg because of the balance the Germans want to maintain between their major *länders*, and the 1986 meeting held in Prime Minister Bettino Craxi's hometown of Milan.

75. Five badges only give access to the meeting room. Two are issued to the main actors. The third nominative badge goes to the permanent representative's assistant who functions as a liaison agent between the principals and the delegation, while two anonymous badges are used by delegations to introduce people in the room when required by one of the principals because of their special expertise or, more often, because of the need to communicate information and instructions. Twelve other badges give access to the delegation rooms but not to the meeting room. And all the others are "technical badges," with access restricted to the building but not to the floors or sections reserved for the meeting and delegation rooms. In some instances, the rest of the delegation is not even granted access to the main building. A transfer system is in operation to allow needed delegation members with technical badges to gain access to the delegation rooms and confer there with the principals or a senior delegation member.

76. One of the three is the head of the Commission's civil service, the secretary general of the Commission. Since the beginning of the EC and until the middle of 1987, there has only been one secretary general, the highly respected Frenchman Emile

Noël – a gentleman, a dedicated European, and a formidable mind in the service of European integration. He has shaped generations of civil servants and outlived every Commission through his encyclopedic knowledge and unswerving habit of gently but firmly pointing out nonsense when he saw it. His recently appointed successor comes from Margaret Thatcher's Cabinet Office. David Williamson starts his new and challenging job with a great capital of sympathy and respect earned through many years' quiet efficiency in dealing with the EC, both inside and outside of the Commission services. That he was chosen, in spite of being British, says a lot about the extent of that respect.

77. Special allowances have always been made for the French delegation because it is led by its head of state and because of its independent nuclear deterrent, which requires a special communications link with the president. The development of "cohabitation" (used by the French to describe the unwilling team of the socialist Mitterrand and the conservative Chirac) has added to the already considerable size of the French delegation, partially calculated to impress on other Europeans the majesty of the office of the president. The British, who also have an independent nuclear deterrent, are more discreet about this and manage with far fewer people. Their prime minister wields the political power, of course, but is not a head of state.

78. The June 1986 European Council, which met in The Hague, gave rise to heated discussions on this issue. Most leaders believed that a political signal of disapproval had to be sent to Pretoria. In addition, the pressure of some for effective – as opposed to symbolic – economic sanctions threatened the major trade links with South Africa that were nurtured by others. To cap it all, the question was raised, and never solved, as to the most likely effect of meaningful sanctions. Would the black South Africans not suffer most? Were they really willing – as some would have it – to put their dignity above their livelihoods? And who were the Europeans anyway to give lessons or to take decisions that would affect them so drastically? As always, some of the expressed doubts masked other preoccupations.

79. Depending on the date of the European Council meeting, there might be room for a "mopping up" meeting of the General Affairs Council under the same Presidency. But that is not always possible, and the next Presidency inherits the bulk of the decisions of the European Council and the task of implementing them.

80. In December 1987, the federalist intergroup of the European Parliament—a pluralist group with the participation of the major political parties present in the Parliament—published an opinion poll it had commissioned in all member states. This was an important step in more ways than one. It was the first such poll to be addressed directly to the European electors, above the heads of the national governments. And the results showed that, in a majority of countries, the electorate was ahead of its national leaders in its desire for greater integration. Among the questions asked were the following:

"Should the European Parliament receive increased legislative powers?"

	Yes	No	?
Belgium	55%	12%	33%
Denmark	17	64	23
Germany	41	33	26
Greece	35	26	39
Spain	48	12	40
France	58	22	20
Ireland	36	35	29
Italy	69	15	16
Luxembourg	45	32	23
Netherlands	50	25	25
Portugal	45	17	38
UK	34	53	13
EC average	49	28	23

"Should there be a European government responsible before the European Parliament? Should the Parliament receive a mandate to draft a European Constitution?"

	For a European Government			For a Mandate		
	Yes	No	?	Yes	No	?
Belgium	55%	12%	33%	61%	6%	33%
Denmark	13	64	23	20	52	28

Germany	41	28	31	58	19	23
Greece	38	21	41	38	15	47
Spain	50	10	40	51	7	42
France	60	19	21	69	6	25
Ireland	39	23	38	41	15	44
Italy	70	11	19	76	4	20
Luxembourg	52	20	28	67	6	27
Netherlands	45	25	30	56	13	31
Portugal	42	14	44	50	5	45
UK	31	45	24	45	26	29
EC average	48	24	28	58	14	28

Other significant questions were put to the public. Ten thousand Europeans were interviewed for this opinion poll conducted by the member institutes of the European Omnibus Survey (Gallup International); the results have been published in the European media.

81. Plenary sessions are held once a month in Strasbourg and last for a week. On Friday mornings, many MEPs depart early for their home constituencies or to attend to other activities. The more disciplined parliamentary groups use this time to push last-minute surprise votes that do not reflect the majority opinion of the Parliament but are nonetheless recorded as such because a majority of the MEPs present at the time voted for it. This can be embarrassing, especially in the case of votes relating to an international issue. Foreign governments are not always aware of this procedural trick, and even when they are, they argue, not incorrectly, that the opinion expressed is publicized as being that of the Parliament, irrespective of the size of the majority that voted for it.

82. The present Council building, known as "the Charlemagne," was designed for six member states. Successive enlargements have forced the secretariat to renovate the building several times, but there always is a limit to the number of meeting rooms large enough to accommodate 14 participants (12 member states, the Commission, and the Presidency). Hapless officials are designated in the Presidency's permanent representation to allot the meeting rooms; tempers sometimes flare between them and fellow civil servants, who are eager to call a meeting on their favorite issue to achieve progress on it and who hope for a breakthrough under their chairmanship. Pressures build up as the Presidency

nears the end of its term, and ministers sometimes intervene in the discussions. Ministerial meetings are also limited in numbers. A new building is being erected in Brussels to accommodate the present and future membership of the EC.

83. Both documents are circulated in all the EC languages.

84. Belgian Foreign Minister Tindemans writes about this in his recent book, *Europa zonder kompas — Reisverhaal van een minister* [Europe without a compass — the travels of a minister] (Antwerp: Standaard Uitgeverij, 1987). In his speech on January 22, 1987, he stated:

> At the start of a new presidency, the atmosphere is usually a bit euphoric. Months pass and the same happens with this pleasant attitude. Eventually, the same president has to report on the accomplishments [of the Presidency] and is compelled to acknowledge that little of what he proposed has been achieved. In spite of this, many will conclude that theirs was a good presidency. Do not expect such language from me. Everything cannot be accomplished in six months. But we shall fight in earnest to bring forward a democratic, dynamic, courageous and more united Europe. [Translation by the author from the original text in Dutch.]

85. The minister is allowed to have two or three aides seated next to him in the Presidency benches.

86. The European Parliament is even more spread out over Europe than the Council. Its secretariat is in Luxembourg while its normal plenary sessions are held in Strasbourg and its commission meetings take place in Brussels. Many MEPs complain about the resulting waste of time, energy, and money, but the matter of sites is officially not theirs to settle — it belongs to the member states. Neither France nor Luxembourg are prepared to give up without a fight the advantages their respective cities derive from the presence of large, well-funded, and prestigious institutions. A majority of MEPs would like to see all activities concentrated in Brussels, home base of the Commission, the Council, and the EPC secretariat. Most of them reside in Brussels because of the importance of the parliamentary commissions' work, the presence of the other EC institutions, and the better air links with the rest of the EC, especially with home constituencies. The Parliament has begun an extensive building program in Brussels to house the commissions, and private developers are build-

ing a new conference center that could accommodate extraordinary plenary sessions of the Parliament if desired.

87. See Schoutheete, "The Presidency and the Management of Political Cooperation," in *European Political Cooperation in the 1980s*.

88. Lord Plumb became famous and popular with dedicated integrationists by his remark shortly after his election that he was born an Englishman, but hoped to die a European.

89. See article 7 of the Single European Act, which replaces article 149 of the EEC Treaty. It provides for a measure of "codecision" that really grants Parliament a second reading and a greater influence over what remains essentially a decision taken by the Council.

90. Differences in organization have often led to delays as bureaucratic infighting took place in the various capitals with different sets of players, adding to the confusion on complex issues. Proposals to remedy this state of affairs have been initiated regularly with no success. One of the ideas most frequently submitted is to introduce a measure of uniformity into the workings of the national bodies responsible for European integration—for example, by making the permanent representative a junior minister with direct access to the cabinet or by replacing the foreign minister with a European minister of cabinet rank. The practice in most countries has been to give the permanent representative easy access to the cabinet or to a ministerial committee, especially at the time of the Presidency. Separating the foreign minister from European matters would mean in effect doing away with a very substantial amount of his present responsibilities and his bureaucratic power base, a development likely to be strenuously resisted by the foreign ministries. As European integration progresses, some of these developments may indeed take place but not in the immediate future.

91. Owing to heavy time constraints, these contacts are also organized in the margins of the first available ministerial meeting and not necessarily in all of the capitals of the other member states.

92. Lobbies proliferate in Brussels, and the time cannot be too far off when lobbyists will be as much a part of Brussels as they are of Washington.

93. The Council picks up the tab for the ministers and some of their assistants traveling on EC business. The Presidency is

also required to coordinate these matters because other Council presidents have legitimate reasons to travel to the other member states – for example, to smooth the way on some tricky decision through personal lobbying with a "difficult" foreign colleague – but the EC budget is limited. EPC travels are paid for by each country as it assumes the presidency.

94. In his 1975 report "European Union," Léo Tindemans called for a one-year Presidency to promote continuity. This provoked negative reactions, even in his own country, because of the tremendous workload involved in running the Presidency, especially for the smaller member state. As the EC expanded, it became difficult to contemplate holding the Presidency only once every 12 years. Too much knowledge would be lost in the process, and most participants would permanently be involved in reinventing the wheel, although this drawback could be lessened with an increased role for the Council Secretariat and the secretariat of the EPC.

The idea is resisted by political leaders out of fear of administrative dominance, but the real problem of half-year cycles remains. The tenure of the Presidency is barely longer than the learning curve. The troika system might be open to further development, and the possibility of another member state taking on tasks on behalf of the Presidency has been debated several times in the past. This idea is already partly at work in foreign countries where the Presidency does not have a diplomatic representative, and another EC member state delegates for it. Also, the EPC expressly provides for the possibility of one member state acting on behalf of the Presidency when continuity of an existing diplomatic action might call for a specific minister to pursue existing contacts or when one member state might be especially well placed to influence a situation to the common advantage because of historic links or some other factor. No use of this has been made so far to the best of my knowledge, but the possibility is there.

95. The few subjects not discussed are mostly agricultural questions, when they are of a technical nature, and some of the more sensitive financial matters.

96. As a consequence, COREPER has in fact become two distinct meetings. One of them is the preserve of the assistant permanent representatives and is known as COREPER 1, simply because it meets on Wednesdays before the ambassadors meet. COREPER 1 deals with complex technical matters, some of

which are eminently political – such as the budget. COREPER 2 is the "nobler" of the two since it is the one in which the ambassadors themselves meet on Thursdays. In case of need, COREPER meetings will be held anywhere and at literally anytime. But Wednesdays and Thursdays have been deliberately chosen because of the national cabinet meeting days in the capitals (they have not been harmonized yet) and the weekly meeting of the Commission, which is on Wednesdays. The job of the Presidency is to ensure perfect coordination between both COREPER meetings and to steer the issues to one or the other. Some countries will strongly prefer one or the other for a variety of reasons that mostly have to do with personalities and calendars.

97. See Declaration of the Twelve on the Middle East, Brussels, February 23, 1987. An outline of its content is in note 59.

98. See note 84.

99. A good question for a revised edition of "Trivial Pursuit" is the order in which the member states take on the Presidency. The answer is the following: Belgium, Denmark, Germany, Greece, Spain, France, Ireland, Italy, Luxembourg, the Netherlands, Portugal, and the United Kingdom. The alphabetical order is set up according to the name of each country in its official language – for example, Greece is "Ellas," and Spain, "España." Spain and Portugal have not yet run a Presidency because they became members in 1986, and the alphabetical rotation was ending with the Netherlands and the United Kingdom that year. The present series started with Belgium in 1987 and will end in 1992, coinciding with the introduction of the internal market. Given that presidencies take on different responsibilities depending on whether the term covers the first or the second half of the year (for example, agricultural prices are decided in the first half, and the budget is adopted in the second half), the member states incorporated an elaborate rotation system in the Single European Act. The next series will not unfold in the traditional fashion. Starting in 1993, a switch will take place between the first and the second half of the year. The 1993 presidencies will be run by Belgium and Denmark, but the order will be reversed, Denmark assuming that responsibility from January to June and passing it on to Belgium after that. In 1994, Germany and Greece will switch, and so on until the end of that series.

100. The ACP countries are nearly all former European colonies linked to the EC by the Lomé convention, which provides

for one of the world's most comprehensive relationships between developing and developed regional groupings. Indeed, the regional approach is the most original feature of this remarkable vehicle for cooperation. For negotiating with the EC, a permanent process because of the regular updating of the Lomé convention and the intervening reviewing conferences, the ACP countries have established a secretariat based in Brussels and several joint institutions.

The EFTA, created by the British as a counterweight to the EEC in the early 1960s, has been much weakened by the UK's later accession to the EC. Purely a free-trade zone with minimal official institutions, the EFTA's present membership comprises Finland, Sweden, Norway, Austria, and Switzerland, with associate status for Iceland. Misgivings are frequently heard from these economically significant countries about their impotence at shaping the policies of its massive EC neighbor, especially now that the single market seems to be a realistic goal for the EC by the end of 1992. Although a free-trade agreement is in place between the EC and EFTA and many consultations are held within existing joint mechanisms, these misgivings are likely to weaken the EFTA further through new defections from it to the EC.

101. These contacts have sometimes been difficult communication exercises. At one time during the disputes about the effects of Spanish accession on the exports of U.S. products, then Secretary of Commerce Malcolm Baldrige left a conference he was attending on the West Coast, got in his car, and used the car phone to talk to Commissioner Willy De Clercq in Brussels.

102. See Moss, "European Community and Transatlantic Relations." To a European, this article is a welcome American echo to preoccupations long held about the state of the overall relationship between the EC and the United States.

103. Finland, long an associate member, has now applied for full membership in a move that reflects Helsinki's steady rapprochement with European institutions and its growing confidence that the Soviet Union will not hinder such moves as long as good relations are maintained between the two countries.

104. The Soviet Union has indeed ended years of aloofness and officially recognized the existence of the EPC by communicating to the Presidency a formal reaction to the statement of the Twelve concerning the proposed International Conference on the Middle East. And an agreement between the EC and COMECON

(Council for Mutual Economic Assistance) was signed in June 1988, which will no doubt be followed by a restatement of the often and informally expressed interest in sustained political dialogue concerning foreign policy. Regular luncheon meetings in Moscow between the ambassadors of the Twelve and the Soviet foreign minister are contemplated.

105. See Tindemans, *Europa zonder kompas*, pp. 105–108.

106. A good example of this can be found in the way the Danish government handled the parliamentary opposition to ratification of the Single European Act. It called for a referendum and won it. Admittedly, the main theme was not the future of European integration and Denmark's role in it but rather whether Denmark could afford not to ratify the act. Nonetheless, the debate did strike at some longer-term European issues.

107. This idea has been introduced by ex-President Giscard d'Estaing of France but in another form. He envisaged a president of the European Council, thus perpetuating the concept of a coalition of states – an intermediate-term possibility.

One question that regularly crops up in this context is that of Europe's monarchies. The EC is evenly divided between republics and constitutional monarchies. Six monarchies (Belgium, Denmark, Spain, Luxembourg, the Netherlands, and the United Kingdom) harmoniously coexist with six republics (Germany, Greece, France, Ireland, Italy, and Portugal). Historic precedents for dealing with that kind of situation can be found in the German Empire of 1871–1918 or, much closer in time, in the present Malaysian Federation with its rotating head of state. The Swiss rotate their ministers, the number of whom is wisely limited to seven.

The directly elected president of Europe could head the executive, and a rotating system of heads of state could be devised. Or he could preside over Europe, each component state retaining its president or monarch for a transitional period that could vary from country to country, depending on the emotional and symbolic weight attached to these functions and their holders.

108. The UK and Denmark have better track records than their fellow member states, probably a reflection of their strong desire to closely monitor potentially unwanted developments.

109. The EPC secretariat will probably have to merge into the Council Secretariat though it should retain its specific functions as a separate division.

Index

www.ingramcontent.com/pod-product-compliance
Lightning Source LLC
Chambersburg PA
CBHW062032270326
41929CB00014B/2413